MW01041312

THE COMPLETE ANTI-INFLAMMATORY DIET PLAN COOKBOOK

2000 Days of Delicious and Nutritious Recipes with a 30-day Meal Plan to Reduce Inflammation and Enhance Immunity

Scott Currey

©Copyright by Scott Currey. All rights reserved.

This document provides exact and reliable information regarding the topic and issues covered. The publication is sold because the publisher is not required to render accounting, officially permitted, or otherwise qualified services. A practiced professional individual should be ordered if advice is necessary, legal, or experienced from a Declaration of Principles accepted and approved equally by a Committee of the American Bar Association and a Committee of Publishers and Associations. It is not legal to reproduce, duplicate, or transmit any part of this document in either electronic means or printed format. Recording this publication is prohibited, and any storage of this document is not allowed unless written permission from the publisher. All rights reserved. The information provided herein is stated to be truthful and consistent in that any liability, in terms of inattention or otherwise, by any usage or abuse of any policies, processes, or directions contained within is the solitary and utter responsibility of the recipient reader. Under no circumstances will any legal obligation or blame be held against the publisher for reparation, damages, or monetary loss due to the information herein, either directly or indirectly. Respective authors own all copyrights not controlled by the publisher. The information herein is solely offered for informational purposes and is universal. The presentation of the data is without a contract or guarantee assurance. The trademarks used are without any consent, and the trademark publication is without permission or backing by the trademark owner. All trademarks and brands within this book are for clarifying purposes only and are owned by the owners, not affiliated with this document.

Table of Contents

Introduction

Are you tired of feeling sluggish, battling chronic pain, or dealing with persistent health issues? Do you yearn for a life filled with vitality, energy, and renewed well-being? If so, you're not alone; we have the perfect solution for you!

In a world where fast-paced lifestyles and processed foods have become the norm, it's no surprise that inflammation-related ailments are rising. The good news? You have the power to take control of your health, and it all begins with what you eat.

Enter our comprehensive and life-transforming «Anti-Inflammatory Diet Plan Cookbook.» This isn't just another cookbook; it's your passport to a vibrant, pain-free, and healthier life. By adopting an anti-inflammatory diet, you can bid farewell to chronic inflammation, the silent culprit behind many common health concerns such as arthritis, heart disease, obesity, and more.

Lasting Results: The «Anti-Inflammatory Diet Plan Cookbook» isn't just a short-term fix. It's a sustainable lifestyle change that will help you look and feel your best for years.

Health Benefits Galore: Following our anti-inflammatory plan, you can expect reduced inflammation, increased energy, improved digestion, better skin, and a strengthened immune system.

Investing in your health is your best decision, and this cookbook is your guide on that journey. Whether you're a seasoned chef or a kitchen novice, our recipes are accessible to everyone. So, why wait any longer to transform your life?

Take the first step towards a healthier, happier you. Grab your copy of the «Anti-Inflammatory Diet Plan Cookbook» today and embark on a journey to wellness that will change your life forever. Your body will thank you, and you'll wonder why you didn't start sooner. Don't wait - your path to optimal health starts here!

Chapter 1

Anti-inflammatory diet

What Exactly Does an Anti-Inflammatory Diet Mean?

In a world where diets often appear like fleeting trends, the Anti-Inflammatory Diet is a lasting and scientifically supported approach to health and well-being. But what exactly does it mean to follow an Anti-Inflammatory Diet, and why has it gained such prominence in nutrition and wellness?

At its core, an Anti-Inflammatory Diet is more than just a set of dietary guidelines; it's a way of life that prioritizes foods known to combat inflammation. But before we delve into the specifics of this transformative dietary approach, let's first understand what inflammation is and why it matters.

Inflammation: What Is It?

Inflammation is a fundamental biological response that is crucial to our body's defense mechanism. When our body perceives a threat, such as an injury or an invading pathogen like bacteria or viruses, it mobilizes its resources to protect and heal itself. This process is known as acute inflammation and is a vital part of our immune system's arsenal.

Think of acute inflammation as a short-lived, controlled fire—a blaze that's purposefully ignited to clear away debris and safeguard our body against harm. It's the reason behind the redness, heat, and swelling we often associate with an injury or infection.

Inflammation: Acute and Chronic

However, when inflammation becomes chronic—lingering in our bodies for weeks, months, or even years—it transitions from a helpful ally into a harmful adversary. Chronic inflammation is now recognized as a critical driver of numerous health issues, including heart disease, diabetes, arthritis, and even certain types of cancer.

The culprits behind chronic inflammation are often lifestyle-related, including poor dietary choices, excessive stress, lack of physical activity, and exposure to environmental toxins. It's this chronic inflammation that the Anti-Inflammatory Diet seeks to address and mitigate.

By carefully selecting foods with known anti-inflammatory properties and eliminating or reducing those that promote inflammation, individuals can help their bodies strike a balance. This balance, in turn, can lead to improved health, increased energy, and a reduced risk of chronic diseases.

Throughout this cookbook, we will guide you to embracing the Anti-Inflammatory Diet, providing delicious recipes that nourish your body and tantalize your taste buds. You'll discover that eating to combat inflammation means something other than sacrificing flavor or satisfaction. It's quite the opposite—it's about savoring the vibrant and diverse world of foods that support your well-being. So, whether you're embarking on this journey as a proactive step towards better health or seeking relief from chronic inflammation-related issues, welcome. The Anti-Inflammatory Diet is more than just a dietary plan; it's an invitation to live your life to the fullest, armed with the knowledge and nourishment to flourish. In the following chapters, we will explore a wide array of recipes, each carefully crafted to help you harness the power of an anti-inflammatory lifestyle.

Treatments for Chronic Inflammation

Inflammation is the body's natural response to injury or infection, but it can lead to various health issues when it becomes chronic. Managing chronic inflammation is crucial for maintaining overall well-being. Here, we explore some treatments commonly used for chronic inflammation.

1. Medications: Nonsteroidal anti-inflammatory drugs (NSAIDs) like ibuprofen and prescription medications can help reduce inflammation and manage pain. However, prolonged use of certain medications may have side effects, so it's essential to consult a healthcare provider.

2. Lifestyle Changes: Modifying lifestyle factors can profoundly impact chronic inflammation. Regular exercise, stress management, and adequate sleep are essential to an anti-inflammatory lifestyle.

3. Dietary Modifications: The most impactful treatment is adopting an Anti-Inflammatory Diet. This dietary approach focuses on consuming foods that help reduce inflammation while avoiding those that promote it. The recipes in this cookbook are designed to support this anti-inflammatory lifestyle.

Foods to Avoid

To effectively combat chronic inflammation, it's equally important to identify and avoid foods that can exacerbate the problem. Some of these inflammatory culprits include:

1. Processed Foods: Highly processed foods often contain trans fats, refined sugars, and artificial additives, which can promote inflammation. Steer clear of these whenever possible.

2. Sugary Drinks: Beverages high in sugar, such as soda and certain fruit juices, can lead to inflammation and other health issues when consumed regularly.

3. Red and Processed Meats: These meats contain saturated fats and advanced glycation end-products (AGEs), which can contribute to inflammation when consumed in excess.

4. Refined Carbohydrates: Foods made from refined grains, such as white bread and pastries, can cause rapid spikes in blood sugar levels, triggering inflammation.

5. Saturated and Trans Fats: These unhealthy fats are often found in fried foods, margarine, and processed snacks. Reducing their intake can help manage inflammation.

Benefits of the Anti-Inflammatory Diet

Adopting an Anti-Inflammatory Diet offers a multitude of benefits that extend far beyond just managing chronic inflammation:

1. Reduced Risk of Chronic Diseases: Numerous studies have shown that this diet may lower the risk of heart disease, diabetes, cancer, and neurodegenerative conditions like Alzheimer's.

2. Weight Management: An anti-inflammatory lifestyle can support healthy weight management, crucial for overall health and inflammation control.

3. Enhanced Energy: Many individuals report increased energy levels and reduced fatigue after transitioning to an anti-inflammatory diet.

4. Improved Gut Health: A diet of anti-inflammatory foods can promote a healthy gut microbiome, closely linked to immune function and overall well-being.

5. Balanced Blood Sugar: This diet can help regulate blood sugar levels, benefitting individuals with diabetes or those at risk.

6. Better Mental Health: Emerging research suggests a connection between the gut and brain health. An anti-inflammatory diet may contribute to improved mood and reduced risk of depression.

As you embark on your journey with the Anti-Inflammatory Diet, you'll discover that it's not just about what you exclude from your meals but about the incredible variety of nutrient-rich, flavorful foods you can include. The recipes in this cookbook are your gateway to a healthier, more vibrant life—a life free from the burden of chronic inflammation and filled with vitality and well-being.

Chapter 2: Breakfast and brunch

Turmeric Scramble

Total Servings: 1 serving
Preparation Time: 5 minutes
Time to Cook: 5 minutes

Ingredients:
- 2 large eggs
- 1/4 teaspoon ground turmeric
- 1/4 teaspoon ground black pepper
- 1/4 teaspoon olive oil
- 2 tablespoons diced tomatoes
- 2 tablespoons chopped fresh cilantro
- Salt to taste

Instructions:

1. Crack the eggs into a bowl and beat them well. Add the ground turmeric and black pepper to the beaten eggs and whisk until the mixture is well combined.

2. Heat a non-stick skillet over medium-low heat. Add the olive oil and swirl it around to coat the pan evenly.

3. Pour the egg mixture into the skillet and let it cook without stirring for a minute or two until the edges begin to set.

4. Using a spatula, gently push and fold the eggs from the edges towards the center. Continue to cook, occasionally moving and folding, until the eggs are mostly set but still slightly runny on top.

5. Add the diced tomatoes to the eggs and continue to cook for another minute or until the eggs are fully cooked, and the tomatoes are heated.

6. Sprinkle the chopped fresh cilantro over the scrambled eggs and gently mix it.

7. Season the scrambled eggs with salt to taste and serve hot.

Per Serving: Calories: 180
Protein: 12g Fat: 14g Salt: 0.3g

Berry Quinoa Bowl

Total Servings: 1 serving
Preparation Time: 10 minutes
Time to Cook: 15 minutes (for quinoa)

Ingredients:
- 1/2 cup cooked quinoa
- 1/2 cup mixed berries (strawberries, blueberries, raspberries)
- 1/4 cup Greek yogurt
- 1 tablespoon honey
- 1 tablespoon chopped almonds
- 1/4 teaspoon vanilla extract
- A pinch of ground cinnamon

Instructions:

1. Start by cooking quinoa according to package instructions. Once cooked, let it cool slightly.

2. Mix the Greek yogurt with honey, vanilla extract, and a pinch of ground cinnamon in a bowl. Stir until well combined.

3. In a serving bowl, add the cooked quinoa as the base.

4. Top the quinoa with the mixed berries.

5. Spoon the sweetened Greek yogurt mixture over the berries and quinoa.

6. Sprinkle the chopped almonds on top for added texture and flavor.

7. You can drizzle a little extra honey over the bowl if desired.

Per Serving: Calories: 350 Protein: 10g
Fat: 6g Salt: 0.2g

Avocado Tomato Toast

Total Servings: 1 serving
Preparation Time: 10 minutes
Time to Cook: N/A

Ingredients:
- 1 slice of whole-grain bread
- 1/2 ripe avocado
- 1/2 small tomato, diced
- 1/4 small red onion, finely chopped
- 1 tablespoon fresh cilantro, chopped
- 1/2 lime, juiced
- Salt and black pepper to taste

Instructions:

1. Toast the whole-grain bread to your desired level of crispiness.

2. Cut the ripe avocado in half while the toast is still warm, remove the pit, and scoop out the flesh. Mash the avocado with a fork in a bowl.

3. Combine the diced tomato, finely chopped red onion, chopped fresh cilantro, and lime juice in another bowl. Mix them well to make a simple tomato salsa.

4. Spread the mashed avocado evenly onto the toasted bread.

5. Top the avocado toast with the tomato salsa.

6. Season with salt and black pepper to taste.

7. Serve immediately, and enjoy your healthy avocado toast with tomato salsa.

Per Serving: Calories: 280 Protein: 5g
Fat: 16g Salt: 0.5g

Green Spinach Smoothie

Total Servings: 1 serving
Preparation Time: 5 minutes
Time to Cook: 0 minutes

Ingredients:
- 1 cup fresh spinach leaves
- 1/2 ripe banana
- 1/2 cup diced pineapple (fresh or frozen)
- 1/2 cup unsweetened almond milk
- 1 tablespoon chia seeds
- 1/2 tablespoon honey (optional)
- Ice cubes (optional)

Instructions:

1. In a blender, combine the fresh spinach leaves, ripe banana, diced pineapple, unsweetened almond milk, chia seeds, and honey (if using).

2. Optionally, add a few ice cubes for a colder and thicker smoothie.

3. Blend all the ingredients on high until the mixture is smooth and creamy. If needed, you can add more almond milk for your desired consistency.

4. Pour the green spinach smoothie into a glass.

5. Serve immediately, and enjoy the refreshing and nutritious goodness.

Per Serving: Calories: 250 Protein: 4g Fat: 6g
Salt: 0.1g

Chia Almond Pudding

Total Servings: 1 serving
Preparation Time: 5 minutes (plus chilling time)
Time to Cook: 0 minutes

Ingredients:
- 3 tablespoons chia seeds
- 1 cup unsweetened almond milk
- 1/2 teaspoon vanilla extract
- 1/2 tablespoon maple syrup (optional)
- 1/4 cup sliced almonds
- Fresh berries (optional, for garnish)

Instructions:

1. In a bowl, combine the chia seeds, unsweetened almond milk, vanilla extract, and maple syrup (if using). Stir well to ensure all ingredients are thoroughly mixed.

2. Cover the bowl and refrigerate for at least 2 hours or overnight, allowing the chia seeds to absorb the liquid and form a pudding-like consistency.

3. After the chia pudding is set, please stir it to fluff it up.

4. Transfer the chia almond pudding into a serving dish.

5. Top with sliced almonds for added texture.

6. Optionally, garnish with fresh berries for a burst of color and flavor.

7. Serve chilled, and enjoy a delightful and nutritious chia almond pudding.

Per Serving: Calories: 320 Protein: 10g Fat: 21g
Salt: 0.1g

Sweet Potato Hash

Total Servings: 1 serving
Preparation Time: 10 minutes
Time to Cook: 15 minutes

Ingredients:
- 1 small sweet potato, peeled and diced
- 1/4 red bell pepper, diced
- 1/4 red onion, finely chopped
- 1 clove garlic, minced
- 1/2 teaspoon paprika
- 1/4 teaspoon ground cumin
- Salt and black pepper to taste
- 1/2 tablespoon olive oil
- Fresh cilantro (optional, for garnish)

Instructions:

1. In a skillet, heat the olive oil over medium heat.

2. Add the diced sweet potato, red bell pepper, red onion, and minced garlic. Sauté for 10 minutes or until the sweet potatoes are tender and slightly crispy.

3. Season with paprika, ground cumin, salt, and black pepper. Stir well to coat the ingredients with the spices evenly.

4. Continue cooking for another 5 minutes, allowing the flavors to meld together.

5. Transfer the sweet potato hash to a serving plate.

6. Optionally, garnish with fresh cilantro for added freshness.

7. Serve hot and savor the deliciousness of your homemade sweet potato hash.

Per Serving: Calories: 35 Protein: 3g Fat: 8g
Salt: 0.2g

Coconut Yogurt Parfait

Total Servings: 1 serving
Preparation Time: 5 minutes
Time to Cook: 0 minutes

Ingredients:

- 1/2 cup unsweetened coconut yogurt
- 1/4 cup fresh mixed berries (e.g., strawberries, blueberries, raspberries)
- 2 tablespoons granola (gluten-free if desired)
- 1 tablespoon honey (optional)
- 1/2 teaspoon chia seeds (optional)
- Fresh mint leaves (optional, for garnish)

Instructions:

1. Start by layering half of the unsweetened coconut yogurt in a glass or serving dish.

2. Add half of the fresh mixed berries on top of the yogurt layer.

3. Sprinkle half of the granola over the berries.

4. Optionally, drizzle honey over the granola for a touch of sweetness.

5. Repeat the layering process with coconut yogurt, mixed berries, and granola.

6. If desired, sprinkle chia seeds over the top layer for texture and nutrition.

7. Optionally, garnish with fresh mint leaves to enhance the presentation.

8. Serve immediately and enjoy this delightful coconut yogurt parfait, perfect for a nutritious and satisfying breakfast or snack.

Per Serving: Calories: 300 Protein: 6g Fat: 8g Salt: 0.1g

Salmon Avocado Wrap

Total Servings: 1 serving
Preparation Time: 15 minutes
Time to Cook: 10 minutes

Ingredients:
- 1 salmon fillet (4-6 ounces)
- 1 whole-grain or gluten-free wrap
- 1/2 avocado, sliced
- 1/4 cup cucumber, thinly sliced
- 1/4 cup mixed greens (e.g., spinach, arugula)
- 1/2 lemon, juiced
- Salt and black pepper to taste
- Olive oil for cooking

Instructions:

1. Preheat a skillet over medium-high heat and add a drizzle of olive oil.

2. Season the salmon fillet with salt and black pepper.

3. Place the salmon fillet skin-side down in the skillet and cook for about 3-4 minutes per side or until it flakes easily with a fork. Squeeze lemon juice over the salmon while cooking.

4. Remove the salmon from the skillet and let it cool slightly. Once cooled, break it into smaller pieces.

5. Lay the whole-grain or gluten-free wrap on a clean surface.

6. Start assembling your wrap by placing the mixed greens in the center of the wrap.

7. Add the sliced avocado, cucumber, and cooked salmon pieces on top of the greens.

8. Carefully fold in the sides of the wrap and then roll it up tightly.

9. Slice the wrap in half diagonally if desir

10. Serve immediately and enjoy this nutritious salmon avocado wrap, packed with anti-inflammatory ingredients and flavor.

Per Serving: Calories: 45 Protein: 25g Fat: 20g Salt: 0.4g

Almond Banana Oats

Total Servings: 1 serving
Preparation Time: 10 minutes
Time to Cook: 5 minutes

Ingredients:
- 1/2 cup rolled oats
- 1 cup unsweetened almond milk
- 1 ripe banana, mashed
- 1 tablespoon almond butter
- 1/2 teaspoon ground cinnamon
- 1/4 teaspoon vanilla extract
- Sliced almonds (optional, for garnish)

Instructions:

1. In a saucepan, combine the rolled oats and unsweetened almond milk.

2. Bring the mixture to a gentle boil over medium heat, stirring occasionally.

3. Reduce the heat to low and simmer for about 3-5 minutes or until the oats are tender and the mixture thickens.

4. Remove the saucepan from heat and stir in the mashed ripe banana, almond butter, ground cinnamon, and vanilla extract. Mix until well combined.

5. Transfer the almond banana oats to a serving bowl.

6. Optionally, garnish with sliced almonds for added crunch and nuttiness.

7. Serve hot, and enjoy this comforting and nutritious bowl of almond banana oats.

Per Serving: Calories: 380 Protein: 9g Fat: 12g Salt: 0.2g

Spinach Mushroom Frittata

Total Servings: 1 serving
Preparation Time: 10 minutes
Time to Cook: 15 minutes

Ingredients:

- 2 large eggs 1/4 cup spinach, chopped
- 1/4 cup mushrooms, sliced
- 2 tablespoons diced onion
- 1/2 teaspoon olive oil
- Salt and black pepper to taste
- Fresh herbs (e.g., parsley or chives, optional, for garnish)

Instructions:

1. In a non-stick skillet, heat the olive oil over medium heat.

2. Add the diced onion and sauté for 2-3 minutes or until it becomes translucent.

3. Add the sliced mushrooms to the skillet and cook for another 2-3 minutes until they soften.

4. Stir in the chopped spinach and cook for 2 minutes until it wilts.

5. In a separate bowl, whisk the eggs until well beaten. Season with a pinch of salt and black pepper.

6. Pour the beaten eggs evenly over the sautéed vegetables in the skillet.

7. Allow the frittata to cook undisturbed for 5-7 minutes until the edges are set and the center is slightly runny.

8. Preheat the broiler in your oven.

9. Place the skillet under the broiler for about 2-3 minutes until the top of the frittata is golden brown and se

10. Carefully remove the skillet from the oven (use an oven mitt), garnish with fresh herbs if desired, and let it cool for a minute.

11. Slide the spinach mushroom frittata onto a plate, slice, and serve hot.

Per Serving: Calories: 220 Protein: 15g Fat: 15g Salt: 0.6g

Mediterranean Breakfast

Total Servings: 1 serving
Preparation Time: 10 minutes
Time to Cook: 0 minutes

Ingredients:

- 1/2 cup Greek yogurt
- 1/4 cup cherry tomatoes, halved
- 2 tablespoons cucumber, diced
- 2 tablespoons Kalamata olives, pitted and sliced
- 1 tablespoon fresh basil, chopped
- 1/2 tablespoon extra-virgin olive oil
- Salt and black pepper to taste

Instructions:

1. In a serving bowl, spoon the Greek yogurt and spread it evenly.

2. Arrange the halved cherry tomatoes, diced cucumber, and sliced Kalamata olives on the yogurt.

3. Sprinkle fresh basil over the vegetables.

4. Drizzle extra-virgin olive oil over the entire bowl.

5. Season with a pinch of salt and black pepper to taste.

6. Gently toss the ingredients together to combine.

7. Serve immediately and enjoy this refreshing Mediterranean-inspired breakfast.

Per Serving: Calories: 280 Protein: 15 Fat: 15g Salt: 0.7g

Blueberry Pancakes

Total Servings: 1 serving (3 small pancakes)
Preparation Time: 10 minutes
Time to Cook: 10 minutes

Ingredients:

- 1/4 cup rolled oats
- 1/4 cup whole-wheat flour
- 1/2 teaspoon baking powder
- 1/4 teaspoon ground cinnamon
- 1/4 cup unsweetened almond milk (or any milk of your choice)
- 1/4 cup fresh blueberries
- 1 tablespoon pure maple syrup (optional for drizzling)
- Cooking spray or a small amount of oil for the pan

Instructions:

1. Combine the rolled oats, whole-wheat flour, baking powder, and ground cinnamon in a mixing bowl.

2. Stir in the almond milk to create a smooth batter. If the batter is too thick, you can add a little more milk.

3. Gently fold in the fresh blueberries.

4. Preheat a non-stick skillet over medium-high heat and lightly grease it with cooking spray or oil.

5. Pour small portions of the batter onto the skillet to form small pancakes. Cook for 2-3 minutes on each side until golden brown.

6. Once the pancakes are cooked through, stack them on a plate.

7. Optionally, drizzle pure maple syrup over the pancakes for added sweetness.

8. Serve hot, and enjoy these wholesome blueberry pancakes as a delightful breakfast treat.

Per Serving: Calories: 320 Protein: 8g Fat: 3g Salt: 0.3g

Cinnamon Quinoa Porridge

Total Servings: 1 serving
Preparation Time: 5 minutes
Time to Cook: 15 minutes

Ingredients:

- 1/2 cup quinoa, rinsed
- 1 cup unsweetened almond milk (or any milk of your choice)
- 1/2 teaspoon ground cinnamon
- 1 tablespoon pure maple syrup (optional for drizzling)
- 1/4 cup fresh mixed berries (e.g., blueberries, strawberries, raspberries)
- 1 tablespoon chopped nuts (e.g., almonds, walnuts)
- Fresh mint leaves for garnish (optional)

Instructions:

1. In a saucepan, combine the rinsed quinoa and almond milk.

2. Bring the mixture to a boil, then reduce the heat to low. Simmer for about 15 minutes, or until the quinoa is cooked and the mixture thickens, stirring occasionally.

3. Stir in the ground cinnamon for added flavor.

4. If desired, drizzle with pure maple syrup for sweetness.

5. Transfer the quinoa porridge to a serving bowl.

6. Top with fresh mixed berries and chopped nuts for added texture and nutrition.

7. Garnish with fresh mint leaves if available.

Per Serving: Calories: 320 Protein: 9g Fat: 7g Salt: 0.3g

Berry Yogurt Mix

Total Servings: 1 serving
Preparation Time: 5 minutes
Time to Cook: 0 minutes

- Ingredients:
- 1/2 cup Greek yogurt
- 1/4 cup fresh mixed berries (e.g., blueberries, strawberries, raspberries)
- 1 tablespoon honey (optional for drizzling)
- 1 tablespoon chia seeds
- 1/4 teaspoon vanilla extract
- 1 tablespoon sliced almonds (optional, for garnish)

Instructions:

1. In a serving bowl, spoon the Greek yogurt.

2. Arrange the fresh mixed berries on top of the yogurt.

3. Drizzle honey over the berries for sweetness (optional).

4. Sprinkle chia seeds over the yogurt and berries.

5. Add a touch of vanilla extract for flavor.

6. Optionally, garnish with sliced almonds for extra crunch.

7. Gently mix the ingredients or enjoy them layered.

Per Serving: Calories: 280 Protein: 15g Fat: 10g Salt: 0.2g

Veggie Burritos

Total Servings: 1 serving
Preparation Time: 10 minutes
Time to Cook: 10 minutes

Ingredients:

- 1 small whole-grain tortilla
- 1/2 cup cooked quinoa (leftover quinoa from the porridge works great)
- 1/4 cup black beans, cooked and drained
- 1/4 cup diced bell peppers (any color)
- 1/4 cup diced tomatoes
- 2 tablespoons diced red onion
- 1/4 teaspoon ground cumin
- 1/4 teaspoon chili powder
- 1/4 avocado, sliced
- Fresh cilantro leaves for garnish (optional)

Instructions:

1. In a mixing bowl, combine the cooked quinoa, black beans, bell peppers, tomatoes, and red onion.

2. Sprinkle ground cumin and chili powder over the mixture for flavor.

3. Lay the whole-grain tortilla flat on a plate or clean surface.

4. Spoon the quinoa and veggie mixture onto the center of the tortilla.

5. Add sliced avocado on top.

6. If desired, garnish with fresh cilantro leaves for added freshness.

7. Fold the sides of the tortilla inward and then roll it up from the bottom to create a burrito.

8. Slice the burrito in half, if preferred, and serve.

Per Serving: Calories: 45 Protein: 15g Fat: 12g Salt: 0.8g

Golden Milk Oats

Total Servings: 1 serving
Preparation Time: 5 minutes
Time to Cook: 10 minutes

Ingredients:

- 1/2 cup rolled oats
- 1 cup unsweetened almond milk (or any milk of your choice)
- 1/2 teaspoon ground turmeric
- 1/4 teaspoon ground cinnamon
- 1 tablespoon honey (or maple syrup for a vegan option)
- 1/4 teaspoon vanilla extract
- 1 tablespoon chopped nuts (e.g., almonds, cashews, or walnuts)
- Fresh berries for garnish (optional)

Instructions:

1. In a saucepan, combine the rolled oats and almond milk.

2. Stir in the ground turmeric and ground cinnamon.

3. Bring the mixture to a gentle boil, then reduce the heat to low. Simmer for about 7-10 minutes, or until the oats are cooked and the mixture thickens, stirring occasionally.

4. Remove from heat and stir in honey (or maple syrup) and vanilla extract for sweetness and flavor.

5. Transfer the golden milk oats to a serving bowl.

6. Top with chopped nuts for added texture and nutrition.

7. Garnish with fresh berries if desired.

Per Serving: Calories: 350 Protein: 9g Fat: 10g Salt: 0.2g

Spinach Tomato Quesadilla

Total Servings: 1 serving
Preparation Time: 10 minutes
Time to Cook: 10 minutes

Ingredients:

- 1 whole-grain tortilla
- 1/2 cup fresh spinach leaves
- 1/4 cup diced tomatoes
- 2 tablespoons diced red onion
- 1/4 cup shredded mozzarella cheese (or dairy-free cheese for a vegan option)
- 1/4 teaspoon dried oregano
- 1/4 teaspoon dried basil
- Cooking spray or olive oil for cooking

Instructions:

1. Lay the whole-grain tortilla flat on a clean surface.

2. On one half of the tortilla, layer the fresh spinach leaves, diced tomatoes, diced red onion, and shredded mozzarella cheese.

3. Sprinkle dried oregano and dried basil over the ingredients for flavor.

4. Fold the other half of the tortilla over to cover the fillings, creating a half-moon shape.

5. Heat a skillet over medium heat and lightly coat it with cooking spray or olive oil.

6. Place the quesadilla in the skillet and cook for about 3-5 minutes on each side until the tortilla is golden brown and the cheese is melted.

7. Remove from heat and let it cool for a minute before slicing.

Per Serving: Calories: 380 Protein: 15g Fat: 14g Salt: 0.8g

Matcha Green Smoothie

Total Servings: 1 serving
Preparation Time: 5 minutes
Time to Cook: 0 minutes

Ingredients:

- 1 cup unsweetened almond milk (or any milk of your choice)
- 1/2 ripe banana
- 1 teaspoon matcha green tea powder
- 1/2 teaspoon honey (optional, for sweetness)
- 1/2 teaspoon vanilla extract
- 1/2 cup fresh spinach leaves
- 1/2 cup frozen mango chunks

Instructions:

1. Combine the unsweetened almond milk, ripe banana, matcha green tea powder, honey (if using), and vanilla extract in a blender.

2. Add the fresh spinach leaves and frozen mango chunks to the blender.

3. Blend until smooth and creamy. Add more almond milk if needed to reach your desired consistency.

4. Taste and adjust sweetness with honey if necessary.

5. Pour the matcha green smoothie into a glass and enjoy immediately.

Per Serving: Calories: 220 Protein: 3 Fat: 2g Salt: 0.2g

Cauliflower Hash Browns

Total Servings: 1 serving
Preparation Time: 15 minutes
Time to Cook: 15 minutes

Ingredients:

- 1 cup grated cauliflower (about half a medium cauliflower head)
- 1/4 cup grated zucchini
- 1 egg
- 1/4 cup almond flour
- 1/4 teaspoon garlic powder
- 1/4 teaspoon onion powder
- Salt and pepper to taste
- Cooking spray or olive oil for cooking

Instructions:

1. Place the grated cauliflower in a clean kitchen towel or cheesecloth. Squeeze out any excess moisture.

2. Combine the grated cauliflower, grated zucchini, egg, almond flour, garlic powder, onion powder, salt, and

pepper in a mixing bowl. Mix well until all ingredients are evenly combined.

3. Heat a skillet over medium heat and lightly coat it with cooking spray or olive oil.

4. Scoop a portion of the cauliflower mixture into the skillet and flatten it to form a hash brown patty. Repeat with the remaining mixture.

5. Cook for 3-4 minutes on each side until the hash browns are golden brown and cooked.

6. Remove from the skillet and place on a paper towel to remove any excess oil.

7. Serve your cauliflower hash browns hot with a side of your favorite anti-inflammatory sauce or salsa.

Per Serving: Calories: 220 Protein: 11 Fat: 15g Salt: 0.4g

Acai Berry Bowl

Total Servings: 1 serving
Preparation Time: 10 minutes
Time to Assemble: 5 minutes

Ingredients:
- 1 unsweetened frozen acai berry packet
- 1/2 cup unsweetened almond milk (or any milk of your choice)
- 1/2 ripe banana
- 1/2 cup mixed berries (strawberries, blueberries, raspberries)
- 1 tablespoon chia seeds
- 1/4 cup granola (choose a low-sugar, whole-grain option)
- Fresh berries and sliced banana for topping (optional)

Instructions:

1. Run the frozen acai berry packet under warm water for a few seconds to soften it slightly.

2. Combine the softened acai berry packet, unsweetened almond milk, ripe banana, and half of the mixed berries in a blender.

3. Blend until you achieve a thick, smoothie-like consistency. You may need to stop and scrape down the sides of the blender to ensure everything is well-mixed.

4. Pour the acai berry mixture into a bowl.

5. If desired, top the acai bowl with the remaining mixed berries, chia seeds, granola, fresh berries, and sliced banana.

6. Serve your delicious acai berry bowl immediately, and enjoy!

Per Serving: Calories: 350 Protein: 8g Fat: 11g Salt: 0.2g

Spinach Feta Omelette

Total Servings: 1 serving
Preparation Time: 10 minutes
Time to Cook: 5 minutes

Ingredients:
- 2 large eggs
- 1/2 cup fresh spinach leaves
- 1/4 cup crumbled feta cheese
- 1/4 teaspoon dried oregano
- Salt and pepper to taste
- Cooking spray or olive oil for cooking

Instructions:

1. Crack te eggs into a bowl and beat them well with a fork or whisk. Season with a pinch of salt and pepper.

2. Heat a non-stick skillet over medium heat and lightly coat it with cooking spray or olive oil.

3. Pour the beaten eggs into the skillet and swirl them around to ensure an even layer.

4. Allow the eggs to cook undisturbed for a minute or until the edges set.

5. Sprinkle the fresh spinach leaves, crumbled feta cheese, and dried oregano evenly over one-half of the omelet.

6. Carefully fold the other half of the omelet over the toppings to create a half-moon shape.

7. Cook for 1-2 minutes or until the omelet is fully set and the cheese is melted.

8. Slide your spinach feta omelet onto a plate and serve immediately.

Per Serving Calories: 290 Protein: 21g Fat: 20g Salt: 0.7g

Almond Pancakes

Total Servings: 1 serving
Preparation Time: 10 minutes
Time to Cook: 10 minutes

Ingredients:
- 1/2 cup almond flour
- 1/4 teaspoon baking powder
- 1 large egg
- 1/4 cup almond milk
- 1/4 teaspoon vanilla extract
- 1 tablespoon honey (optional)
- A pinch of salt
- Cooking spray or olive oil for cooking

Instructions:

1. In a mixing bowl, combine the almond flour and baking powder.

2. Whisk together the egg, almond milk, vanilla extract, honey (if using), and a pinch of salt in a separate bowl.

3. Pour the wet ingredients into the dry ingredients and stir until you have a smooth batter.

4. Heat a non-stick skillet or griddle over medium heat and lightly coat it with cooking spray or olive oil.

5. Pour 1/4 cup of the pancake batter onto the skillet for each pancake.

6. Cook the pancakes for 2-3 minutes on each side or until golden brown and cooked through.

7. Remove the almond pancakes from the skillet and serve immediately. You can drizzle some honey or top with fresh berries for added flavor.

Per Serving: Calories: 350 Protein: 14g Fat: 26g Salt: 0.2g

Tofu Breakfast Tacos

Total Servings: 1 serving
Preparation Time: 15 minutes
Time to Cook: 10 minutes

Ingredients:
- 2 small corn or whole-grain tortillas
- 1/2 cup extra-firm tofu, crumbled
- 1/4 cup diced bell peppers
- 1/4 cup diced tomatoes
- 2 tablespoons diced red onion
- 1/2 teaspoon turmeric powder
- 1/4 teaspoon cumin powder
- Salt and pepper to taste
- Cooking spray or olive oil for cooking
- Fresh cilantro and lime wedges for garnish (optional)

Instructions:

1. Heat a non-stick skillet with a bit of cooking spray or olive oil over medium heat.

2. Add the diced red onion and bell peppers to the skillet and sauté for 2-3 minutes until they soften.

3. Stir in the crumbled tofu and cook for another 2-3 minutes.

4. Add the turmeric and cumin powder to the mixture, stirring well to coat the tofu evenly. Season with salt and pepper to taste.

5. Warm the tortillas in the skillet or microwave for about 30 seconds.

6. Spoon the tofu mixture into the tortillas.

7. If desired, top with diced tomatoes and garnish with fresh cilantro and lime wedges.

8. Serve your delicious tofu breakfast tacos immediately.

Per Serving: Calories: 32 Protein: 18g Fat: 12g Salt: 0.5g

Mango Turmeric Blend

Total Servings: 1 serving
Preparation Time: 5 minutes

Ingredients:
- 1 ripe mango, peeled and diced
- 1/2 cup unsweetened almond milk (or any milk of your choice)
- 1/2 teaspoon turmeric powder
- 1/4 teaspoon ground ginger
- 1/2 teaspoon honey (optional)
- Ice cubes (optional)

Instructions:

1. Place the diced mango, almond milk, turmeric powder, ground ginger, and honey (if using) in a blender.

2. If you prefer a colder drink, add a few ice cubes.

3. Blend until you have a smooth and creamy mango-turmeric blend.

4. Pour your refreshing mango turmeric blend into a glass.

5. Serve immediately and enjoy the vibrant flavors and anti-inflammatory benefits.

Per Serving: Calories: 180 Protein: 2g Fat: 1g Salt: 0.1g

Zucchini Casserole

Total Servings: 1 serving
Preparation Time: 15 minutes
Time to Cook: 30 minutes

Ingredients:
- 1 small zucchini, thinly sliced
- 1/2 cup cherry tomatoes, halved
- 1/4 cup diced red onion
- 1/4 cup diced bell peppers (any color)
- 1 clove garlic, minced
- 1/4 cup grated Parmesan cheese (optional)
- 1/2 teaspoon dried oregano
- 1/2 teaspoon dried basil
- Salt and pepper to taste
- Olive oil for drizzling

Instructions:

1. Preheat your oven to 350°F (175°C).

2. In a small baking dish or casserole dish, layer the thinly sliced zucchini, halved cherry tomatoes, diced red onion, and diced bell peppers.

3. Sprinkle the minced garlic evenly over the vegetables.

4. Mix the dried oregano, dried basil, and a pinch of salt and pepper in a small bowl.

5. Sprinkle the herb mixture over the vegetables.

6. If desired, sprinkle the grated Parmesan cheese on top for added flavor.

7. Drizzle a bit of olive oil over the casserole.

8. Cover the dish with foil and bake for about 20-25 minutes or until the vegetables are tender.

9. Remove the foil and bake for 5-10 minutes until the top is slightly golden

10. Let it cool for a few minutes before serving your delicious zucchini casserole.

Per Serving: Calories: 180 Protein: 8g Fat: 8g
Salt: 380mg

Almond Butter Sandwich

Total Servings: 1 serving
Preparation Time: 5 minutes

Ingredients:
- 2 slices whole-grain bread (or gluten-free bread if preferred)
- 2 tablespoons almond butter (unsweetened)
- 1/2 banana, sliced
- 1 teaspoon honey (optional)
- A pinch of cinnamon (optional)

Instructions:

1. Toast the whole-grain bread slices until they are golden brown.

2. Spread almond butter evenly on both slices of bread.

3. Arrange the banana slices on one slice of bread.

4. Drizzle honey and sprinkle a pinch of cinnamon over the banana slices if desired.

5. Place the other slice of bread on top to form a sandwich.

6. Slice in half if preferred, and your almond butter sandwich is ready to enjoy.

Per Serving: Calories: 380 Protein: 9g Fat: 17g Salt: 250mg

Quinoa Kale Bowl

Total Servings: 1 serving
Preparation Time: 20 minutes
Time to Cook: 15 minutes

Ingredients:
- 1/2 cup cooked quinoa
- 1 cup chopped kale leaves
- 1/4 cup chickpeas (cooked or canned)
- 1/4 cup diced cucumber
- 1/4 cup diced red bell pepper
- 2 tablespoons lemon-tahini dressing (see instructions below)
- Lemon-tahini dressing ingredients:
- 1 tablespoon tahini
- 1 tablespoon lemon juice

- 1 tablespoon water
- 1 clove garlic, minced
- Salt and pepper to taste

Instructions:

1. Cook quinoa according to package instructions and set aside.

2. Prepare the lemon-tahini dressing by whisking together tahini, lemon juice, water, minced garlic, salt, and pepper until smooth.

3. In a mixing bowl, massage the chopped kale with a drizzle of the lemon-tahini dressing until it softens.

4. Add the cooked quinoa, chickpeas, cucumber, and red bell pepper to the bowl.

5. Drizzle the remaining lemon-tahini dressing over the ingredients.

6. Toss everything together until well combined.

7. Serve your nutritious quinoa kale bowl immediately.

Per Serving:
Calories: 380
Protein: 12g
Fat: 12g
Salt: 320mg

Anti-Inflammatory Burrito

Total Servings: 1 serving
Preparation Time: 15 minutes
Time to Cook: 10 minutes

Ingredients:
- 1 whole-grain or gluten-free tortilla
- 1/2 cup cooked quinoa
- 1/4 cup black beans (cooked or canned), drained and rinsed
- 1/4 cup diced avocado
- 1/4 cup diced tomatoes
- 1/4 cup diced red bell pepper
- 1/4 cup shredded kale leaves
- 1/4 teaspoon ground turmeric
- 1/4 teaspoon ground cumin
- Salt and pepper to taste

Instructions:

1. Combine the cooked quinoa, black beans, turmeric, ground cumin, and a pinch of salt and pepper in a small bowl. Mix well to incorporate the spices.

2. Lay the tortilla flat on a clean surface.

3. Spread the quinoa and black bean mixture evenly onto the center of the tortilla.

4. Top the mixture with diced avocado, tomatoes, red bell pepper, and shredded kale leaves.

5. Carefully fold in the sides of the tortilla, then roll it up tightly from the bottom to create a burrito.

6. Heat a non-stick skillet over medium heat. Place the burrito seam-side on the skillet and cook for about 3-5 minutes on each side until it s lightly browned and crispy.

7. Remove the burrito from the skillet, let it cool slightly, then slice it in half if preferred.

8. Your anti-inflammatory burrito is ready to be served.

Per Serving: Calories: 420 Protein: 10g Fat: 10g Salt: 340mg

Coconut Chia Mango

Total Servings: 1 serving
Preparation Time: 5 minutes (plus chilling time)
Time to Cook: None

Ingredients:
- 1/2 cup unsweetened coconut milk
- 2 tablespoons chia seeds
- 1/2 teaspoon vanilla extract
- 1 teaspoon honey (optional)
- 1/2 ripe mango, diced

Instructions:

1. In a small bowl, combine the unsweetened coconut milk, chia seeds, vanilla extract, and honey (if desired). Stir well to mix.

2. Cover the bowl and refrigerate for at least 2 hours or overnight to let the chia seeds thicken and absorb the liquid.

3. Once the chia pudding has set, please give it a good stir.

4. Layer the diced mango and coconut chia pudding in a serving glass or bowl.

5. If desired, drizzle a little extra honey on top for sweetness.

6. Your refreshing coconut chia mango dessert is ready to enjoy.

Per Serving: Calories: 320 Protein: 6g Salt: 15g Salt: 40mg

Spinach Pepper Muffins

Total Servings: 1 serving (2 muffins)
Preparation Time: 15 minutes
Time to Cook: 20 minutes

Ingredients:
- 1/2 cup gluten-free flour (or whole-grain flour if preferred)
- 1/2 teaspoon baking powder
- 1/4 teaspoon baking soda
- 1/4 teaspoon ground turmeric
- 1/4 teaspoon ground black pepper
- 1/4 cup unsweetened almond milk
- 1/2 cup fresh spinach, chopped
- 1/4 cup diced red bell pepper
- 1/4 cup diced onion

- Cooking spray (for greasing the muffin tin)

Instructions:

1. Preheat your oven to 350°F (175°C). Grease a muffin tin with cooking spray or line it with muffin liners.

2. Combine the gluten-free flour, baking powder, baking soda, ground turmeric, and ground black pepper in a mixing bowl. Mix well.

3. Add the unsweetened almond milk to the dry ingredients and stir until a batter forms.

4. Fold in the chopped fresh spinach, red bell pepper, and diced onion.

5. Spoon the muffin batter evenly into the tin, filling each cup about 2/3 full.

6. Bake in the preheated oven for about 18-20 minutes or until a toothpick inserted into the center of a muffin comes out clean.

7. Let the muffins cool in the tin for a few minutes, then transfer them to a wire rack to cool completely.

8. Your spinach pepper muffins are now ready to be enjoyed.

Per Serving (2 Muffins): Calories: 220 Protein: 5g Fat: 2g Salt: 360mg

Chapter 3: Meat

Grilled Lemon Herb Chicken

Total Servings: 1 serving
Preparation Time: 10 minutes
Time to Cook: 15 minutes

Ingredients:
- 1 boneless, skinless chicken breast (about 6 oz)
- 1 lemon, juiced and zested
- 1 tablespoon fresh rosemary, chopped
- 1 clove garlic, minced
- 1 tablespoon olive oil
- Salt and pepper to taste

Instructions:

1. In a small bowl, combine the lemon juice, lemon zest, fresh rosemary, minced garlic, olive oil, salt, and pepper to create a marinade.

2. Place the chicken breast in a resealable plastic bag and pour the marinade over it. Seal the bag and massage the marinade into the chicken. Let it marinate in the refrigerator for at least 30 minutes.

3. Preheat your grill or grill pan over medium-high heat.

4. Remove the chicken from the marinade, allowing any excess to drip off, and grill for 6-8 minutes per side or until the chicken is cooked through and no longer pink in the center. The internal temperature should reach 165°F (74°C).

5. Remove the grilled chicken from the heat and let it rest for a few minutes before slicing it.

6. Serve your grilled lemon herb chicken with your choice of anti-inflammatory side dishes.

Per Serving: Calories: 280 Protein: 36g Fat: 13g Salt: 450mg

Garlic Rosemary Lamb Chops

Total Servings: 1 serving
Preparation Time: 10 minutes
Time to Cook: 12-15 minutes

Ingredients:
- 2 lamb chops
- 1 clove garlic, minced
- 1 tablespoon fresh rosemary, chopped
- 1 tablespoon olive oil
- Salt and pepper to taste

Instructions:

1. Combine the minced garlic, fresh rosemary, olive oil, salt, and pepper in a small bowl to create a marinade.

2. Rub the marinade over both sides of the lamb chops and let them marinate at room temperature for about 15 minutes.

3. Preheat your grill or grill pan over medium-high heat.

4. Place the lamb chops on the grill and cook for about 6-8 minutes per side for medium-rare, or longer if you prefer them more well-done.

5. Remove the lamb chops from the grill and let them rest for a few minutes before serving.

6. Enjoy your garlic rosemary lamb chops with anti-inflammatory side dishes.

Per Serving: Calories: 450 Protein: 30g Fat: 36g Salt: 220mg

Turmeric Glazed Salmon

Total Servings: 1 serving
Preparation Time: 5 minutes
Time to Cook: 12-15 minutes

Ingredients:
- 1 salmon fillet (about 6 oz)
- 1/2 teaspoon ground turmeric
- 1 tablespoon honey
- 1/2 tablespoon olive oil
- Salt and pepper to taste
- Lemon wedges for serving (optional)

Instructions:

1. Preheat your oven to 375°F (190°C).

2. Mix the ground turmeric, honey, olive oil, salt, and pepper in a small bowl to create the glaze.

3. Place the salmon fillet on a baking sheet lined with parchment paper.

4. Brush the salmon generously with turmeric glaze.

5. Bake the salmon in the oven for about 12-15 minutes or until the salmon flakes easily with a fork and has a golden glaze.

6. Remove the salmon from the oven and let it rest for a minute.

7. Serve your turmeric glazed salmon with a squeeze of lemon juice if desired and complement anti-inflammatory side dishes.

Per Serving: Calories: 380 Protein: 36g Fat: 20g Salt: 250mg

Beef Stir-Fry with Ginger

Total Servings: 1 serving
Preparation Time: 10 minutes
Time to Cook: 15 minutes

Ingredients:

- 4 oz beef sirloin, thinly sliced
- 1 tablespoon low-sodium soy sauce (or tamari for gluten-free)
- 1/2 teaspoon fresh ginger, minced
- 1 clove garlic, minced
- 1/2 cup broccoli florets
- 1/2 cup bell peppers, sliced
- 1/2 cup snap peas
- 1/2 tablespoon olive oil
- Salt and pepper to taste
- Red pepper flakes (optional, for added heat)

Instructions:

1. Mix the soy sauce, minced ginger, and minced garlic in a small bowl. This will be your stir-fry sauce.

2. Heat the olive oil in a non-stick skillet or wok over medium-high heat.

3. Add the thinly sliced beef to the hot skillet and stir-fry for about 2-3 minutes or until it s browned but still slightly pink in the center. Remove the meat from the skillet and set it aside.

4. Add broccoli florets, bell peppers, and snap peas in the same skillet. Stir-fry for about 4-5 minutes or until the vegetables are tender-crisp.

5. Return the cooked beef to the skillet and pour the stir-fry sauce over the meat and vegetables. Toss everything together for 1-2 minutes to heat the beef through.

6. Season with salt, pepper, and red pepper flakes if you prefer some heat.

7. Transfer your beef stir-fry with ginger to a plate and enjoy your anti-inflammatory meal!

Per Serving: Calories: 280 Protein: 26g Fat: 13g Salt: 650mg

Balsamic Turkey Tenderloin

Total Servings: 1 servi
Preparation Time: 5 minutes
Time to Cook: 20-25 minutes

Ingredients:

- 1 turkey tenderloin (about 6 oz)
- 1 tablespoon balsamic vinegar
- 1/2 tablespoon olive oil
- 1/2 teaspoon dried rosemary
- Salt and pepper to taste

Instructions:

1. Preheat your oven to 375°F (190°C).

2. Mix the balsamic vinegar, olive oil, dried rosemary, salt, and pepper in a small bowl to create a marinade.

3. Place the turkey tenderloin on a baking sheet lined with parchment paper.

4. Brush the turkey generously with the balsamic marinade.

5. Bake the turkey in the preheated oven for about 20-25 minutes or until it reaches an internal temperature of 165°F (74°C) and is no longer pink in the center.

6. Remove the turkey from the oven and let it rest for a few minutes before slicing.

7. Serve your balsamic turkey tenderloin with anti-inflammatory side dishes.

Per Serving: Calories: 290 Protein: 45g Fat: 8g Salt: 220mg

Mediterranean Shrimp Skewers

Total Servings: 1 serving
Preparation Time: 15 minutes
Time to Cook: 10 minutes

Ingredients:

- 6 large shrimp, peeled and deveined
- 1/2 lemon, juiced and zested
- 1 clove garlic, minced
- 1/2 teaspoon dried oregano
- 1/2 tablespoon olive oil
- Salt and pepper to taste
- 1/4 cup cherry tomatoes
- 1/4 cup red onion, cut into chunks
- 1/4 cup bell peppers, cut into chunks
- Wooden skewers, soaked in water for 30 minutes

Instructions:

1. Mix the lemon juice, lemon zest, minced garlic, dried oregano, olive oil, salt, and pepper in a small bowl to create a marinade.

2. Thread the shrimp onto the wooden skewers, alternating with cherry tomatoes, red onion chunks, and bell pepper chunks.

3. Brush the shrimp and vegetable skewers with the marinade.

4. Preheat your grill or grill pan over medium-high heat.

5. Grill the skewers for about 3-4 minutes per side or until the shrimp turns pink and opaque.

6. Remove the Mediterranean shrimp skewers from the grill and serve with anti-inflammatory side dishes.

Per Serving: Calories: 250 Protein: 25g Fat: 8g Salt: 380mg

Pork Tenderloin with Chutney

Total Servings: 1 serving
Preparation Time: 10 minutes
Time to Cook: 20 minutes

Ingredients:

- 1 pork tenderloin (about 6 oz)
- 2 tablespoons mango chutney
- 1/2 teaspoon ground cumin
- 1/2 teaspoon ground coriander
- Salt and pepper to taste
- 1/2 tablespoon olive oil
- Fresh cilantro leaves (optional, for garnish)

Instructions:

1. Preheat your oven to 375°F (190°C).

2. Mix the mango chutney, ground cumin, coriander, salt, and pepper in a small bowl. This will be your chutney glaze.

3. Heat olive oil in an oven-safe skillet over medium-high heat.

4. Season the pork tenderloin with salt and pepper.

5. Sear the pork tenderloin on all sides until it s nicely browned, about 3-4 minutes per side.

6. Brush the chutney glaze evenly over the seared pork.

7. Transfer the skillet to the preheated oven and roast for approximately 15-20 minutes or until the pork reaches an internal temperature of 145°F (63°C).

8. Remove the pork from the oven, tent it with aluminum foil, and let it rest for a few minutes.

9. Slice the pork tenderloin into medallions, garnish with fresh cilantro leaves if desired, and serve your anti-inflammatory meal.

Per Serving: Calories: 320 Protein: 30g Fat: 10g Salt: 380mg

Spiced Turkey Lettuce Wraps

Total Servings: 1 serving
Preparation Time: 15 minutes
Time to Cook: 10 minutes

Ingredients:

- 4 oz ground turkey
- 1/2 teaspoon ground cumin
- 1/2 teaspoon ground coriander
- 1/4 teaspoon chili powder
- Salt and pepper to taste
- 1/4 cup diced red bell pepper
- 1/4 cup diced cucumber
- 1/4 cup diced tomato
- 1/4 cup diced red onion
- 1/4 avocado, diced
- 1 tablespoon fresh cilantro, chopped
- 2 large lettuce leaves (such as iceberg or butterhead)

Instructions:

1. Over medium heat, cook the ground turkey in a skillet until it›s browned and cooked through, breaking it into small crumbles with a spoon as it cooks.

2. Add the ground cumin, coriander, chili powder, salt, and pepper to the cooked turkey. Stir well to incorporate the spices. Remove from heat.

3. Combine the diced red bell pepper, cucumber, tomato, red onion, avocado, and fresh cilantro in a small bowl. This will be your fresh salsa.

4. Place two large lettuce leaves on a plate.

5. Spoon the spiced ground turkey mixture into the lettuce leaves.

6. Top with the fresh salsa.

7. Serve your spiced turkey lettuce wraps as a healthy and anti-inflammatory meal.

Per Serving: Calories: 320n Protein: 26g Fat: 15g Salt: 450mg

Herbed Chicken Skillet

Total Servings: 1 serving
Preparation Time: 10 minutes
Time to Cook: 15 minutes

Ingredients:

- 1 boneless, skinless chicken breast (about 6 oz)
- 1/2 teaspoon dried thyme
- 1/2 teaspoon dried rosemary
- 1/2 teaspoon dried oregano
- Salt and pepper to taste
- 1/2 tablespoon olive oil
- 1/4 cup low-sodium chicken broth
- 1/2 lemon, juiced
- Fresh parsley leaves (optional, for garnish)

Instructions:

1. Season the chicken breast with dried thyme, rosemary, oregano, salt, and pepper.

2. Heat olive oil in a skillet over medium-high heat.

3. Add the seasoned chicken breast to the hot skillet and cook for about 5-7 minutes per side or until it s no longer pink in the center and reaches an internal temperature of 165°F (74°C).

4. Remove the chicken from the skillet and set it aside.

5. In the same skillet, add low-sodium chicken broth and lemon juice. Please bring it to a simmer, scraping any browned bits from the bottom of the skillet.

6. Return the chicken to the skillet and spoon the sauce over it. Cook for 2-3 minutes, allowing the chicken to absorb the

flavors.

7. Garnish with fresh parsley leaves if desired, and serve your herbed chicken skillet as part of your anti-inflammatory diet.

Per Serving: Calories: 28 Protein: 40g Fat: 10g Salt: 350mg

Lemon Pepper Tuna

Total Servings: 1 serving
Preparation Time: 10 minutes
Time to Cook: 5 minutes

Ingredients:
- 4 oz tuna steak
- 1/2 teaspoon lemon pepper seasoning
- 1/2 tablespoon olive oil
- 1 lemon wedge (for garnish)
- Salt to taste
- Fresh parsley leaves (optional, for garnish)

Instructions:

1. Season the tuna steak with lemon pepper seasoning and a pinch of salt.

2. Heat olive oil in a skillet over high heat.

3. Place the seasoned tuna steak in the hot skillet and cook for about 2-3 minutes per side or until it s seared on the outside and still slightly pink in the center (or to your preferred level of doneness).

4. Remove the tuna steak from the skillet and let it rest for a minute.

5. Squeeze the lemon wedge over the tuna for extra flavor.

6. Garnish with fresh parsley leaves if desired.

7. Serve your lemon pepper tuna as a delicious and anti-inflammatory meal.

Per Serving: Calories: 250 Protein: 30g Fat: 13g Salt: 200mg

Cumin Bison Burger

Total Servings: 1 serving
Preparation Time: 15 minutes
Time to Cook: 10 minutes

Ingredients:
- 4 oz ground bison meat
- 1/2 teaspoon ground cumin
- 1/2 teaspoon ground coriander
- Salt and pepper to taste
- 1 whole-grain burger bun (or lettuce wrap for a lower-carb option)
- Lettuce, tomato, and onion slices for topping (optional)

Instructions:

1. Mix the ground bison meat with ground cumin, coriander,

salt, and pepper in a bowl. Form the mixture into a burger patty.

2. Heat a grill or skillet over medium-high heat.

3. Cook the bison burger patty for about 4-5 minutes per side or until it reaches your preferred level of doneness.

4. Toast the whole-grain burger bun on the grill or in a toaster until lightly browned.

5. If desired, place the cooked bison patty on the bun and add lettuce, tomato, and onion slices.

6. Serve your cumin bison burger as a flavorful and anti-inflammatory meal.

Per Serving: Calories: 350 Protein: 26g Fat: 16g Salt: 450mg

Ginger Pork Ribs

Total Servings: 1 serving
Preparation Time: 10 minutes
Time to Cook: 30 minutes

Ingredients:
- 4 pork ribs
- 1/2 teaspoon ground ginger
- 1/2 teaspoon ground paprika
- 1/4 teaspoon garlic powde
- 1/4 teaspoon onion powder
- Salt and pepper to taste
- 1/2 tablespoon olive oil

Instructions:

1. Mix the ground ginger, paprika, garlic powder, onion powder, salt, and pepper in a bowl to create a spice rub.

2. Rub the spice mixture evenly over the pork ribs. Cover and let them marinate in the refrigerator for at least 30 minutes (or overnight for deeper flavor).

3. Preheat your grill to medium-high heat.

4. Brush the pork ribs with olive oil.

5. Grill the ribs for about 15 minutes per side or until they are cooked through and have grill marks.

6. Remove the ribs from the grill and let them rest for a few minutes.

7. Serve your ginger pork ribs as a flavorful and anti-inflammatory meal.

Per Serving: Calories: 420 Protein: 28g Fat: 32g Salt: 300mg

Cod with Tomato Relish

Total Servings: 1 serving
Preparation Time: 10 minutes
Time to Cook: 15 minutes

Ingredients: 4 oz cod fillet
- 1/2 cup cherry tomatoes, halved
- 1 clove garlic, minced
- 1 tablespoon fresh basil, chopped

- 1/2 tablespoon olive oil
- Salt and pepper to taste
- Lemon wedges for garnish (optional)

Instructions:

1. In a bowl, combine the cherry tomatoes, minced garlic, fresh basil, olive oil, salt, and pepper to create the tomato relish.

2. Season the cod fillet with a pinch of salt and pepper.

3. Heat a skillet over medium-high heat and add a touch of olive oil.

4. Place the cod fillet in the skillet and cook for about 3-4 minutes on each side until it flakes easily with a fork and is opaque throughout.

5. While the cod is cooking, spoon the tomato relish over the top.

6. Once the cod is done, transfer it to a plate and spoon more tomato relish.

7. Garnish with lemon wedges if desired.

8. Serve your cod with tomato relish as a flavorful and anti-inflammatory meal.

Per Serving: Calories: 250 Protein: 26g Fat: 9g Salt: 300mg

Moroccan Chicken Thighs

Total Servings: 1 serving
Preparation Time: 15 minutes
Time to Cook: 20 minutes

Ingredients:

- 2 boneless, skinless chicken thighs
- 1/2 teaspoon ground cumin
- 1/2 teaspoon ground coriander
- 1/4 teaspoon ground cinnamon
- 1/4 teaspoon ground paprika
- Salt and pepper to taste
- 1/2 tablespoon olive oil
- 1/4 cup plain Greek yogurt (optional for serving)

Instructions:

1. Mix the ground cumin, coriander, cinnamon, paprika, salt, and pepper in a bowl to create a spice rub.

2. Rub the spice mixture evenly over both sides of the chicken thighs. Cover and let them marinate in the refrigerator for at least 30 minutes (or longer for enhanced flavor).

3. Preheat your grill or skillet over medium-high heat.

4. Brush the chicken thighs with olive oil.

5. Grill the chicken thighs for about 8-10 minutes per side or until they are cooked through and have grill marks.

6. Remove the chicken thighs from the grill or skillet and let

them rest for a few minutes.

7. If desired, serve your Moroccan chicken thighs with a dollop of plain Greek yogurt.

Per Serving: Calories: 350 Protein: 34g Fat: 16g Salt: 350mg

Stuffed Portobello Mushrooms

Total Servings: 1 serving
Preparation Time: 15 minutes
Time to Cook: 25 minutes

Ingredients:

- 2 large Portobello mushrooms, stems removed
- 1/4 cup quinoa, cooked
- 1/4 cup diced bell peppers (any color)
- 2 tablespoons diced red onion
- 1 clove garlic, minced
- 1/4 teaspoon dried thyme
- Salt and pepper to taste
- 1/4 cup grated Parmesan cheese (optional for topping)
- Fresh parsley leaves for garnish (optional)

Instructions:

1. Preheat your oven to 375°F (190°C).

2. Mix the cooked quinoa, bell peppers, red onion, minced garlic, dried thyme, salt, and pepper to create the stuffing mixture in a bowl.

3. Lightly brush the outside of the Portobello mushrooms with olive oil and season with a pinch of salt and pepper.

4. Fill each mushroom cap with the quinoa stuffing mixture.

5. If desired, sprinkle grated Parmesan cheese on top of the stuffed mushrooms.

6. Place the stuffed mushrooms on a baking sheet and bake for about 20-25 minutes or until the mushrooms are tender and the stuffing is heated through.

7. Garnish with fresh parsley leaves if desired.

8. Serve your stuffed Portobello mushrooms as a delicious and anti-inflammatory meal.

Per Serving: Calories: 300 Protein: 14g Fat: 6g Salt: 500mg

Spicy Chili-Lime Prawns

Total Servings: 1 serving
Preparation Time: 15 minutes
Time to Cook: 5 minutes

Ingredients:

- 6 large prawns (shrimp), peeled and deveined
- Zest and juice of 1 lime

- 1 tablespoon olive oil
- 1 clove garlic, minced
- 1/2 teaspoon chili powder
- 1/4 teaspoon paprika
- Salt and pepper to taste
- Fresh cilantro leaves for garnish (optional)

Instructions:

1. Combine the lime zest, lime juice, olive oil, minced garlic, chili powder, paprika, salt, and pepper to create the marinade.

2. Place the prawns in a resealable plastic bag or a shallow dish, and pour the marinade over them. Seal the bag or cover the dish and refrigerate for at least 30 minutes to allow the flavors to meld.

3. Preheat your grill or skillet over medium-high heat.

4. Remove the prawns from the marinade, letting any excess drip off.

5. Grill or cook the prawns for about 2-3 minutes per side or until they are opaque and cooked through.

6. Remove the prawns from the grill or skillet.

7. Garnish with fresh cilantro leaves if desired.

8. Serve your spicy chili-lime prawns as a delightful and anti-inflammatory meal.

Per Serving: Calories: 200 Protein: 20g Fat: 10g Salt: 200mg

Curry Lamb Kebabs

Total Servings: 1 serving
Preparation Time: 20 minutes
Time to Cook: 10 minutes

Ingredients:
- 4 oz lamb cubes
- 1/2 teaspoon curry powder
- 1/4 teaspoon ground cumin
- 1/4 teaspoon ground coriander
- 1/4 teaspoon ground turmeric
- Salt and pepper to taste
- 1/2 tablespoon olive oil
- Lemon wedges for garnish (optional)

Instructions:

1. Mix the curry powder, ground cumin, coriander, turmeric, salt, and pepper in a bowl to create the spice blend.

2. Thread the lamb cubes onto a skewer.

3. Rub the spice blend evenly onto the lamb kebabs.

4. Heat your grill or skillet over medium-high heat and brush it with olive oil.

5. Grill or cook the lamb kebabs for about 3-4 minutes per side or until they reach your desired level of doneness.

6. Remove the lamb kebabs from the grill or skillet.

7. Garnish with lemon wedges if desired.

8. Serve your curry lamb kebabs as a flavorful and anti-inflammatory meal.

Per Serving: Calories: 350 Protein: 25g Fat: 26g Salt: 350mg

Mustard Pork Loin

Total Servings: 1 serving
Preparation Time: 10 minutes
Time to Cook: 20 minutes

Ingredients:
- 4 oz pork loin
- 1 tablespoon Dijon mustard
- 1/2 tablespoon olive oil
- 1/2 teaspoon dried thyme
- Salt and pepper to taste
- Fresh rosemary sprig for garnish (optional)

Instructions:

1. Mix the Dijon mustard, olive oil, dried thyme, salt, and pepper in a bowl to create the marinade.

2. Coat the pork loin with the marinade, ensuring it›s evenly covered. Marinate in the refrigerator for at least 30 minutes.

3. Preheat your grill or skillet over medium-high heat.

4. Remove the pork loin from the marinade, letting any excess drip off.

5. Grill or cook the pork loin for about 8-10 minutes per side or until it reaches your desired level of doneness.

6. Remove the pork loin from the grill or skillet.

7. Garnish with a fresh rosemary sprig if desired.

8. Serve your mustard pork loin as a delectable and anti-inflammatory meal.

Per Serving: Calories: 300 Protein: 30g Fat: 18g Salt: 300mg

Teriyaki Turkey Meatballs

Total Servings: 1 serving
Preparation Time: 15 minutes
Time to Cook: 20 minutes

Ingredients:
- 4 oz ground turkey
- 1/4 cup breadcrumbs (gluten-free if needed)
- 1/2 teaspoon grated fresh ginger
- 1/2 teaspoon minced garlic
- 2 tablespoons low-sodium teriyaki sauce
- 1 tablespoon chopped green onions
- 1/2 tablespoon olive oil
- Sesame seeds for garnish (optional)

Instructions:

1. Combine the ground turkey, breadcrumbs, grated ginger, minced garlic, and chopped green onions in a mixing bowl.

2. Form the mixture into meatballs about 1 inch in diameter.

3. In a skillet, heat the olive oil over medium heat.

4. Add the turkey meatballs to the skillet and cook for about 5-7 minutes, turning occasionally, until they are browned and cooked.

5. Drizzle the teriyaki sauce over the meatballs and gently toss to coat. Cook for 2-3 minutes until the sauce thickens and glazes the meatballs.

6. Transfer the teriyaki turkey meatballs to a serving plate and sprinkle with sesame seeds if desired.

7. Serve your teriyaki turkey meatballs hot as a savory and anti-inflammatory meal.

Per Serving: Calories: 35 Protein: 25g Fat: 15g Salt: 500mg

Lemon Dill Whitefish

Total Servings: 1 serving
Preparation Time: 10 minutes
Time to Cook: 12 minutes

Ingredients:
- 4 oz whitefish fillet (such as cod or haddock)
- 1 tablespoon fresh lemon juice
- 1/2 teaspoon lemon zest
- 1/2 teaspoon dried dill
- Salt and pepper to taste
- 1/2 tablespoon olive oil
- Fresh dill sprig for garnish (optional)

Instructions:

1. Preheat your oven to 375°F (190°C).

2. Mix the fresh lemon juice, lemon zest, dried dill, salt, and pepper in a small bowl to create the seasoning.

3. Place the whitefish fillet on a baking sheet lined with parchment paper.

4. Brush the fillet with olive oil, ensuring it s coated evenly.

5. Drizzle the lemon seasoning over the fillet.

6. Bake the whitefish in the oven for 10-12 minutes or until it flakes easily with a fork.

7. Transfer the lemon dill whitefish to a serving plate and garnish with a fresh dill sprig if desired.

8. Serve your lemon dill whitefish hot as a light and anti-inflammatory meal.

Per Serving: Calories: 200 Protein: 30g Fat: 7 Salt: 300mg

BBQ Pulled Chicken

Total Servings: 1 serving
Preparation Time: 10 minutes
Time to Cook: 20 minutes

Ingredients:
- 4 oz boneless, skinless chicken breast
- 1/4 cup sugar-free BBQ sauce
- 1/2 tablespoon olive oil
- 1/2 teaspoon smoked paprika
- 1/4 teaspoon garlic powder
- Salt and pepper to taste
- Coleslaw mix for garnish (optional)

Instructions:

1. Combine the sugar-free BBQ sauce, olive oil, smoked paprika, garlic powder, salt, and pepper in a bowl to create the marinade.

2. Place the chicken breast in a resealable plastic bag or a shallow dish, and pour the marinade over it. Seal the bag or cover the dish and refrigerate for at least 30 minutes to marinate.

3. Preheat your grill or skillet over medium-high heat.

4. Remove the chicken breast from the marinade, letting any excess drip off.

5. Grill or cook the chicken breast for 5-7 minutes per side or until it›s cooked through and has grill marks.

6. Remove the chicken breast from the grill or skillet and let it rest for a few minutes.

7. Use two forks to shred the chicken into pulled pieces.

8. Serve your BBQ-pulled chicken with a side of coleslaw mix if desired.

9. Enjoy your BBQ-pulled chicken as a flavorful and anti-inflammatory meal.

Per Serving: Calories: 300 Protein: 25g Fat: 12g Salt: 500mg

Paprika Garlic Drumsticks

Total Servings: 1 serving
Preparation Time: 10 minutes
Time to Cook: 25 minutes

Ingredients:
- 2 chicken drumsticks
- 1/2 teaspoon smoked paprika
- 1/2 teaspoon garlic powder
- 1/2 teaspoon olive oil
- Salt and pepper to taste
- Fresh parsley for garnish (optional)

Instructions:

1. Preheat your oven to 425°F (220°C).

2. Mix the smoked paprika, garlic powder, olive oil, salt, and pepper in a small bowl to create a seasoning paste.

3. Place the chicken drumsticks on a baking sheet lined with parchment paper.

4. Rub the seasoning paste evenly over the drumsticks, ensuring they are well coated.

5. Bake the drumsticks in the oven for approximately 20-25 minutes or until the chicken is cooked and the skin is crispy.

6. Garnish your paprika garlic drumsticks with fresh parsley if desired.

7. Serve hot as a flavorful and anti-inflammatory meal.

Per Serving: Calories: 250 Protein: 30g Fat: 13g Salt: 300mg

Mediterranean Beef Skewers

Total Servings: 1 serving
Preparation Time: 15 minutes
Time to Cook: 10 minutes

Ingredients:
- 4 oz lean beef (such as sirloin or tenderloin), cut into 1-inch cubes
- 1/2 teaspoon dried oregano
- 1/2 teaspoon dried thyme
- 1/2 teaspoon olive oil
- 1/2 teaspoon minced garlic
- Juice of 1/2 lemon
- Salt and pepper to taste
- Cherry tomatoes and red onion wedges for skewering
- Fresh parsley for garnish (optional)

Instructions:

1. Combine the dried oregano, dried thyme, olive oil, minced garlic, lemon juice, salt, and pepper to create the marinade in a bowl.

2. Place the beef cubes in a resealable plastic bag or a shallow dish, and pour the marinade over them. Seal the bag or cover the dish and refrigerate for at least 30 minutes to marinate.

3. Preheat your grill or grill pan over medium-high heat.

4. Thread the marinated beef cubes onto skewers, alternating with cherry tomatoes and red onion wedges.

5. Grill the beef skewers for approximately 5 minutes on each side or until the beef reaches your desired level of doneness and has grill marks.

6. Remove the skewers from the grill.

7. Garnish your Mediterranean beef skewers with fresh parsley if desired.

8. Serve hot as a delicious and anti-inflammatory meal.

Per Serving: Calories: 300 Protein: 25g Fat: 10g Salt: 400mg

Orange Glazed Quail

Total Servings: 1 serving\
Preparation Time: 10 minutes
Time to Cook: 20 minutes

Ingredients:
- 2 quail, split in half
- 1/4 cup freshly squeezed orange juice
- 1/2 teaspoon grated orange zest
- 1/2 teaspoon honey (optional)
- 1/4 teaspoon ground cumin
- 1/4 teaspoon ground coriander
- Salt and pepper to taste
- 1/2 teaspoon olive oil
- Orange slices for garnish (optional)

Instructions:

1. In a bowl, combine the freshly squeezed orange juice, grated orange zest, honey (if used), ground cumin, coriander, salt, and pepper to create the marinade.

2. Place the quail halves in a resealable plastic bag or a shallow dish, and pour the marinade over them. Seal the bag or cover the dish and refrigerate for at least 30 minutes to marinate.

3. Preheat your grill or grill pan over medium-high heat.

4. Remove the quail halves from the marinade, letting any excess drip off.

5. Brush the quail halves with olive oil.

6. Grill the quail halves for approximately 8-10 minutes, turning occasionally, until they are cooked through and have grill marks.

7. Remove the quail halves from the grill.

8. Garnish your orange glazed quail with orange slices if desired.

9. Serve hot as an exquisite and anti-inflammatory meal.

Per Serving: Calories: 250 Protein: 25g Fat: 15g Salt: 400mg

Garlic-Herb Flank Steak

Total Servings: 1 serving
Preparation Time: 10 minutes
Time to Cook: 10 minutes

Ingredients:
- 4 oz flank steak
- 1 clove garlic, minced
- 1/2 teaspoon dried rosemary
- 1/2 teaspoon dried thyme

- 1/2 teaspoon olive oil
- Juice of 1/2 lemon
- Salt and pepper to taste
- Fresh rosemary for garnish (optional)

Instructions:

1. Combine the minced garlic, rosemary, dried thyme, olive oil, lemon juice, salt, and pepper in a bowl to create the marinade.

2. Place the flank steak in a resealable plastic bag or a shallow dish, and pour the marinade over it. Seal the bag or cover the dish and refrigerate for at least 30 minutes to marinate.

3. Preheat your grill or grill pan over medium-high heat.

4. Remove the flank steak from the marinade, letting any excess drip off.

5. Grill the flank steak for approximately 4-5 minutes on each side or until it reaches your desired level of doneness and has grill marks.

6. Remove the flank steak from the grill.

7. Let it rest briefly before slicing it thinly against the grain.

8. Garnish your garlic-herb flank steak with fresh rosemary if desired.

9. Serve hot as a savory and anti-inflammatory meal.

Per Serving: Calories: 250 Protein: 25g Fat: 15g Salt: 400mg

Szechuan Pepper Beef

Total Servings: 1 serving
Preparation Time: 15 minutes
Time to Cook: 10 minutes

Ingredients:

- 4 oz beef sirloin, thinly sliced
- 1/2 teaspoon Szechuan peppercorns, crushed
- 1/2 teaspoon minced ginger
- 1/2 teaspoon minced garlic
- 1/2 teaspoon sesame oil
- 1/2 teaspoon low-sodium soy sauce
- 1/4 teaspoon red pepper flakes (adjust to your preferred spice level)
- 1/2 teaspoon olive oil
- Chopped scallions for garnish (optional)

Instructions:

1. Combine the crushed Szechuan peppercorns, minced ginger, minced garlic, sesame oil, low-sodium soy sauce, and red pepper flakes to create the marinade.

2. Add the thinly sliced beef to the marinade, ensuring it›s well coated, and let it sit for 10 minutes.

3. Heat olive oil in a skillet over medium-high heat.

4. Add the marinated beef to the skillet and cook for 2-3 minutes per side or until it›s cooked to your desired level of doneness.

5. Remove the beef from the skillet.

6. Garnish your Szechuan pepper beef with chopped scallions if desired.

7. Serve hot as a flavorful and anti-inflammatory meal.

Per Serving: Calories: 300 Protein: 25g Fat: 20g Salt: 400mg

Lemon Thyme Turkey

Total Servings: 1 serving
Preparation Time: 10 minutes
Time to Cook: 15 minutes

Ingredients:

- 4 oz turkey breast
- 1/2 teaspoon dried thyme
- 1/2 teaspoon olive oil
- Juice of 1/2 lemon
- Zest of 1/2 lemon
- Salt and pepper to taste
- Fresh thyme for garnish (optional)

Instructions:

1. Combine the dried thyme, olive oil, lemon juice, lemon zest, salt, and pepper in a bowl to create the marinade.

2. Place the turkey breast in a resealable plastic bag or a shallow dish, and pour the marinade over it. Seal the bag or cover the dish and refrigerate for at least 30 minutes to marinate.

3. Preheat your grill or grill pan over medium-high heat.

4. Remove the turkey breast from the marinade, letting any excess drip off.

5. Grill the turkey breast for approximately 6-8 minutes on each side or until it›s cooked through and has grill marks.

6. Remove the turkey breast from the grill.

7. Let it rest for a few minutes before slicing it.

8. Garnish your lemon thyme turkey with fresh thyme if desired.

9. Serve hot as a zesty and anti-inflammatory meal.

Per Serving: Calories: 200 Protein: 25g Fat: 10g Salt: 350mg

Coconut Curry Shrimp

Total Servings: 1 serving
Preparation Time: 15 minutes
Time to Cook: 10 minutes

Ingredients:

- 4 oz large shrimp, peeled and deveined
- 1/2 cup coconut milk (canned, unsweetened)
- 1/2 teaspoon curry powder
- 1/2 teaspoon turmeric powder

- 1/2 teaspoon minced garlic
- 1/2 teaspoon minced ginger
- 1/2 teaspoon olive oil
- Salt and pepper to taste
- Fresh cilantro for garnish (optional)
- Lime wedges for serving

Instructions:

1. Combine the coconut milk, curry powder, turmeric powder, minced garlic, ginger, olive oil, salt, and pepper to create the marinade in a bowl.

2. Add the peeled and deveined shrimp to the marinade, ensuring they are well coated. Allow them to marinate for at least 30 minutes in the refrigerator.

3. Preheat a skillet over medium-high heat.

4. Remove the shrimp from the marinade, letting any excess drip off.

5. Cook the shrimp on each side for 2-3 minutes until they turn pink and opaque.

6. Transfer the cooked shrimp to a serving plate.

7. Garnish with fresh cilantro, and serve with lime wedges for an extra flavor.

8. Enjoy your coconut curry shrimp as a delicious and anti-inflammatory meal.

Per Serving: Calories: 220 Protein: 20g Fat: 15g Salt: 300mg

Spiced Lamb Lettuce Cups

Total Servings: 1 serving
Preparation Time: 15 minutes
Time to Cook: 10 minutes

Ingredients:

- 4 oz ground lamb
- 1/2 teaspoon cumin
- 1/2 teaspoon coriander
- 1/4 teaspoon cinnamon
- 1/2 teaspoon olive oil
- 1/2 teaspoon minced garlic
- 1/2 teaspoon minced ginger
- Salt and pepper to taste
- Iceberg or butter lettuce leaves for serving
- Chopped mint and cilantro for garnish (optional)
- Sliced cucumber for serving

Instructions:

1. Combine the ground lamb, cumin, coriander, cinnamon, olive oil, minced garlic, ginger, salt, and pepper to create the lamb mixture. Allow it to marinate for at least 30

minutes in the refrigerator.

2. Heat a skillet over medium-high heat.

3. Add the marinated lamb mixture to the skillet and cook, breaking it apart with a spoon, for about 4-5 minutes or until it's browned and cooked.

4. Transfer the cooked lamb to a serving plate.

5. Serve the spiced lamb in iceberg or butter lettuce leaves, creating lettuce cups.

6. Garnish with chopped mint and cilantro, and serve with sliced cucumber for a refreshing touch.

7. Enjoy your spiced lamb lettuce cups as a flavorful and anti-inflammatory meal.

Per Serving: Calories: 300 Protein: 20g Fat: 24g Salt: 400mg

Dijon Pork Chops

Total Servings: 1 serving
Preparation Time: 10 minutes
Time to Cook: 15 minutes

Ingredients:

- 1 boneless pork chop (4 oz)
- 1/2 tablespoon Dijon mustard
- 1/2 teaspoon olive oil
- 1/2 teaspoon dried thyme
- 1/2 teaspoon minced garlic
- Salt and pepper to taste
- Fresh parsley for garnish (optional)

Instructions:

1. Combine the Dijon mustard, olive oil, dried thyme, minced garlic, salt, and pepper in a bowl to create the marinade.

2. Place the boneless pork chop in a resealable plastic bag or a shallow dish, and pour the marinade over it. Seal the bag or cover the dish and refrigerate for at least 30 minutes to marinate.

3. Preheat your grill or grill pan over medium-high heat.

4. Remove the pork chop from the marinade, letting any excess drip off.

5. Grill the pork chop for about 4-5 minutes on each side or until it reaches your desired level of doneness.

6. Transfer the cooked pork chop to a serving plate.

7. Garnish with fresh parsley if desired.

8. Enjoy your Dijon pork chop as a tasty and anti-inflammatory meal.

Per Serving: Calories: 250 Protein: 25g Fat: 15g Salt: 350mg

Chapter 4: Poult

Herb-Roasted Chicken

Total Servings: 1 serving
Preparation Time: 10 minutes
Time to Cook: 45 minutes

Ingredients:
- 1 bone-in, skin-on chicken breast (6 oz)
- 1/2 tablespoon olive oil
- 1/2 teaspoon dried rosemary
- 1/2 teaspoon dried thyme
- 1/2 teaspoon dried oregano
- 1/2 teaspoon minced garlic
- Salt and pepper to taste
- Fresh parsley for garnish (optional)
- Lemon wedges for serving

Instructions:

1. In a small bowl, combine the olive oil, rosemary, thyme, oregano, minced garlic, salt, and pepper to create the herb mixture.

2. Gently lift the skin of the chicken breast and rub the herb mixture evenly underneath the skin.

3. Place the chicken breast in a resealable plastic bag or a shallow dish, and refrigerate for at least 30 minutes to marinate.

4. Preheat your oven to 375°F (190°C).

5. Remove the chicken breast from the marinade and place it on a baking sheet lined with parchment paper.

6. Roast the chicken in the oven for about 35-40 minutes or until the internal temperature reaches 165°F (74°C) and the skin is golden and crispy.

7. Transfer the roasted chicken breast to a serving plate.

8. Garnish with fresh parsley, and serve with lemon wedges for added flavor.

9. Enjoy your herb-roasted chicken as a delicious and anti-inflammatory meal.

Per Serving: Calories: 300 Protein: 30g Fat: 18g Salt: 400mg

Lemon Garlic Roast Turkey

Total Servings: 1 serving
Preparation Time: 15 minutes (
Time to Cook: 1 hour

Ingredients:
- 1 turkey thigh (6 oz)
- 1/2 tablespoon olive oil
- 1/2 lemon, juiced and zested
- 1/2 teaspoon dried thyme
- 1/2 teaspoon minced garlic
- Salt and pepper to taste
- Fresh rosemary for garnish (optional)
- Lemon wedges for serving

Instructions:

1. Combine the olive oil, lemon juice, lemon zest, dried thyme, minced garlic, salt, and pepper in a small bowl to create the marinade.

2. Place the turkey thigh in a resealable plastic bag or a shallow dish and pour the marinade over it. Seal the bag or cover the dish and refrigerate for at least 30 minutes to marinate.

3. Preheat your oven to 375°F (190°C).

4. Remove the turkey thigh from the marinade and place it on a baking sheet lined with parchment paper.

5. Roast the turkey in the preheated oven for about 50-60 minutes or until the internal temperature reaches 165°F (74°C) and the skin is golden and crispy.

6. Transfer the roasted turkey thigh to a serving plate.

7. Garnish with fresh rosemary, and serve with lemon wedges for added zing.

8. Enjoy your lemon garlic roast turkey as a flavorful and anti-inflammatory meal.

Per Serving: Calories: 280 Protein: 28g Fat: 16g Salt: 350mg

Orange Ginger Glazed Duck

Total Servings: 1 serving
Preparation Time: 15 minutes
Time to Cook: 1 hour and 15 minutes

Ingredients:
- 1 duck leg (6 oz)
- 1/2 orange, juiced and zested
- 1/2 tablespoon grated fresh ginger
- 1/2 teaspoon minced garlic
- 1/2 teaspoon olive oil
- Salt and pepper to taste
- Fresh cilantro for garnish (optional)
- Orange slices for serving

Instructions:

1. Combine the orange juice, orange zest, grated ginger, minced garlic, olive oil, salt, and pepper in a small bowl to create the marinade.

2. Place the duck leg in a resealable plastic bag or a shallow dish, and pour the marinade over it. Seal the bag or cover the dish and refrigerate for at least 30 minutes to marinate.

3. Preheat your oven to 375°F (190°C).

4. Remove the duck leg from the marinade and place it on a baking sheet lined with parchment paper.

5. Roast the duck in the oven for about 1 hour and 15 minutes or until the skin is crispy and the internal temperature reaches 165°F (74°C).

6. Transfer the roasted duck leg to a serving plate.

7. Garnish with fresh cilantro, and serve with orange slices for a citrusy flavor.

8. Enjoy your orange ginger glazed duck as an exquisite and anti-inflammatory meal.

Per Serving: Calories: 320 Protein: 26g Fat: 22g Salt: 400mg

Cilantro-Lime Chicken Thighs

Total Servings: 1 serving
Preparation Time: 10 minutes
Time to Cook: 25 minutes

Ingredients:
- 2 boneless, skinless chicken thighs (4 oz each)
- 1 lime, juiced and zested
- 1/4 cup fresh cilantro, chopped
- 1/2 teaspoon minced garlic
- 1/2 teaspoon olive oil
- Salt and pepper to taste
- Lime wedges for serving (optional)

Instructions:

1. In a small bowl, combine the lime juice, lime zest, chopped cilantro, minced garlic, olive oil, salt, and pepper to create the marinade.

2. Place the chicken thighs in a resealable plastic bag or a shallow dish, and pour the marinade over them. Seal the bag or cover the dish and refrigerate for at least 30 minutes to marinate.

3. Preheat your grill or a grill pan to medium-high heat.

4. Remove the chicken thighs from the marinade and grill for about 10-12 minutes per side, or until the internal temperature reaches 165°F (74°C) and the chicken is cooked through with grill marks.

5. Transfer the grilled chicken thighs to a serving plate.

6. Garnish with additional cilantro and lime wedges if desired.

7. Enjoy your cilantro-lime chicken thighs as a zesty and anti-inflammatory meal.

Per Serving: Calories: 280 Protein: 30g Fat: 14g Salt: 450mg

Balsamic-Honey Glazed Quail

Total Servings: 1 serving
Preparation Time: 10 minutes
Time to Cook: 20 minutes

Ingredients:
- 2 quail (4 oz each)
- 1/4 cup balsamic vinegar
- 1 tablespoon honey
- 1/2 teaspoon minced garlic
- 1/2 teaspoon olive oil
- Salt and pepper to taste
- Fresh thyme for garnish (optional)

Instructions:

1. Combine the balsamic vinegar, honey, minced garlic, olive oil, salt, and pepper in a small bowl to create the glaze.

2. Place the quail in a resealable plastic bag or a shallow dish, and pour half of the glaze over them. Reserve the other half for later.

3. Seal the bag or cover the dish and refrigerate for at least 30 minutes to marinate.

4. Preheat your grill or a grill pan to medium-high heat.

5. Remove the quail from the marinade and grill for 8-10 minutes per side, basting with the reserved glaze during grilling. Cook until the internal temperature reaches 165°F (74°C) and the quail is cooked.

6. Transfer the grilled quail to a serving plate.

7. Garnish with fresh thyme if desired.

8. Enjoy your balsamic-honey glazed quail as a sweet and savory anti-inflammatory meal.

Per Serving: Calories: 260 Protein: 28g Fat: 12g Salt: 400mg

Mango Turkey Burgers

Total Servings: 1 serving
Preparation Time: 15 minutes
Time to Cook: 12 minutes

Ingredients:
- 1 turkey burger patty (4 oz)
- 1/4 cup fresh mango, diced
- 1/4 teaspoon minced garlic
- 1/4 teaspoon olive oil
- Salt and pepper to taste
- Whole-grain bun (optional)
- Lettuce, tomato, and onion for garnish (optional)

Instructions:

1. Preheat your grill or a grill pan to medium-high hea

2. Brush the turkey burger patty with olive oil and season with salt and pepper.

3. Grill the turkey burger patty for about 5-6 minutes per side or until the internal temperature reaches 165°F (74°C) and the burger is cooked.

4. While the burger is cooking, combine the diced mango and minced garlic in a small bowl. Set aside.

5. Once the turkey burger is cooked, transfer it to a plate.

6. Top the turkey burger with the mango salsa.

7. If desired, serve the burger on a whole-grain bun and garnish with lettuce, tomato, and onion.

8. Enjoy your mango turkey burger as a juicy and anti-inflammatory meal.

Per Serving: Calories: 290 (excluding bun and garnish) Protein: 24g Fat: 16g Salt: 350mg

Rosemary Roast Cornish Hens

Total Servings: 1 serving
Preparation Time: 10 minutes
Time to Cook: 50 minutes

Ingredients:
- 1 Cornish hen (about 1 lb)
- 1 tablespoon olive oil
- 1 teaspoon fresh rosemary, minced
- 1/2 teaspoon minced garlic
- Salt and pepper to taste
- Fresh rosemary sprigs for garnish (optional)
- Lemon wedges for serving (optional)

Instructions:

1. Preheat your oven to 375°F (190°C).

2. Mix the olive oil, minced rosemary, garlic, salt, and pepper in a small bowl to create a marinade.

3. Place the Cornish hen in a resealable plastic bag or a shallow dish, and rub the marinade all over it, ensuring it›s evenly coated. Marinate for at least 30 minutes in the refrigerator.

4. Transfer the marinated Cornish hen to a roasting pan.

5. Roast the Cornish hen in the preheated oven for about 45-50 minutes, or until the internal temperature reaches 165°F (74°C) and the skin is golden and crispy.

6. Remove the Cornish hen from the oven and let it rest for a few minutes.

7. Garnish with fresh rosemary sprigs and serve with lemon wedges if desired.

8. Enjoy your rosemary roast Cornish hen as a flavorful and anti-inflammatory meal.

Per Serving: Calories: 500 Protein: 40g Fat: 35g Salt: 600mg

Lemongrass Coconut Curry

Total Servings: 1 serving
Preparation Time: 15 minutes
Time to Cook: 25 minutes

Ingredients:
- 1 boneless, skinless chicken thigh (4 oz), diced (optional)
- 1/2 cup coconut milk (canned, full-fat)
- 1 lemongrass stalk, smashed and cut into pieces
- 1/2 teaspoon minced garlic
- 1/2 teaspoon minced ginger
- 1/4 cup red bell pepper, sliced
- 1/4 cup zucchini, sliced
- 1/4 cup broccoli florets
- 1/4 cup cauliflower florets
- 1/2 teaspoon curry powder
- 1/2 teaspoon turmeric powder
- Salt and pepper to taste
- Fresh cilantro leaves for garnish (optional)

Instructions:

1. In a medium-sized skillet, heat the coconut milk over medium-low heat. Add the lemongrass pieces and simmer for about 5 minutes, allowing the lemongrass flavor to infuse into the coconut milk. Remove and discard the lemongrass pieces.

2. Add the minced garlic and ginger to the coconut milk and stir for a minute.

3. If using chicken, add the diced chicken thigh to the skillet and cook until it›s no longer pink and cooked through.

4. Stir in the red bell pepper, zucchini, broccoli, and cauliflower. Cook for about 5-7 minutes until the vegetables are tender.

5. Add the curry powder, turmeric powder, salt, and pepper. Stir well to coat the ingredients with the spices.

6. Simmer for an additional 5 minutes to allow the flavors to meld.

7. Transfer the Lemongrass Coconut Curry to a serving bowl.

8. Garnish with fresh cilantro leaves if desired.

9. Enjoy your Lemongrass Coconut Curry as a fragrant and anti-inflammatory meal.

Per serving (without chicken): Calories: 230 Protein: 3g Fat: 20g Salt: 50mg

Garlic-Herb Drumsticks

Total Servings: 1 serving
Preparation Time: 10 minutes
Time to Cook: 30 minutes

Ingredients:
- 2 chicken drumsticks (about 4 oz each)
- 1 teaspoon minced garlic
- 1 teaspoon fresh rosemary, minced
- 1/2 teaspoon olive oil
- Salt and pepper to taste
- Lemon wedges for serving (optional)

Instructions:

1. Preheat your oven to 375°F (190°C).

2. Combine the minced garlic, rosemary, olive oil, salt, and pepper in a small bowl to create a marinade.

3. Place the chicken drumsticks in a resealable plastic bag or a shallow dish, and rub the marinade over them, ensuring they're evenly coated. Marinate for at least 30 minutes in the refrigerator.

4. Transfer the marinated chicken drumsticks to a baking sheet lined with parchment paper.

5. Bake the chicken drumsticks in the preheated oven for about 25-30 minutes, or until the internal temperature reaches 165°F (74°C) and the skin is crispy.

6. Remove the drumsticks from the oven and let them rest for a few minutes.

7. Serve with lemon wedges if desired.

8. Enjoy your garlic-herb drumsticks as a savory and anti-inflammatory meal.

Per Serving: Calories: 300 Protein: 22g Fat: 21g Salt: 400mg

Tarragon Roast Game Hens

Total Servings: 1 serving
Preparation Time: 15 minutes
Time to Cook: 45 minutes

Ingredients:
- 1 Cornish game hen (about 1 lb)
- 1 teaspoon olive oil
- 1 teaspoon fresh tarragon leaves, minced
- 1/2 teaspoon minced garlic
- Salt and pepper to taste
- Fresh tarragon sprigs for garnish (optional)
- Lemon wedges for serving (optional)

Instructions:

1. Preheat your oven to 375°F (190°C).

2. Mix the olive oil, minced tarragon, garlic, salt, and pepper in a small bowl to create a marinade.

3. Place the Cornish game hen in a resealable plastic bag or a shallow dish, and rub the marinade all over it, ensuring its evenly coated. Marinate for at least 30 minutes in the refrigerator.

4. Transfer the marinated Cornish game hen to a roasting pan.

5. Roast the game hen in the oven for about 40-45 minutes, or until the internal temperature reaches 165°F (74°C) and the skin is golden and crispy.

6. Remove the game hen from the oven and let it rest for a few minutes.

7. Garnish with fresh tarragon sprigs and serve with lemon wedges if desired.

8. Enjoy your tarragon roast Cornish game hen as a flavorful and anti-inflammatory meal.

Per Serving: Calories: 450 Protein: 40g Fat: 30g Salt: 500mg

Chili-Lime Turkey Skewers

Total Servings: 1 serving
Preparation Time: 15 minutes
Time to Cook: 15 minutes

Ingredients:
- 1 turkey tenderloin (about 6 oz), cut into cubes
- 1 tablespoon olive oil
- 1 teaspoon chili powder
- 1/2 teaspoon lime zest
- 1 tablespoon fresh lime juice
- Salt and pepper to taste
- Wooden skewers, soaked in water for 30 minutes
- Lime wedges for serving (optional)

Instructions:

1. Combine the olive oil, chili powder, lime zest, lime juice, salt, and pepper in a bowl to create a marinade.

2. Thread the turkey cubes onto the soaked wooden skewers.

3. Brush the turkey skewers with the marinade, ensuring they're evenly coated. Marinate for at least 30 minutes in the refrigerator.

4. Preheat a grill or grill pan to medium-high heat.

5. Grill the turkey skewers for 6-8 minutes per side or until they are cooked through and have grill marks.

6. Remove from the grill and let them rest for a few minutes.

7. Serve with lime wedges if desired.

8. Enjoy your chili-lime turkey skewers as a zesty and anti-inflammatory meal.

Per Serving: Calories: 250 Protein: 30g Fat: 12g Salt: 400mg

Apricot Glazed Chicken Wings

Total Servings: 1 serving
Preparation Time: 10 minutes
Time to Cook: 40 minutes

Ingredients:

- 4-5 chicken wings (about 4 oz), separated into flats and drumettes
- 2 tablespoons apricot jam (no sugar added)
- 1 teaspoon olive oil
- 1/2 teaspoon minced garlic
- Salt and pepper to taste
- Fresh cilantro leaves for garnish (optional)

Instructions:

1. Mix the apricot jam, olive oil, minced garlic, salt, and pepper in a small bowl to create a glaze.

2. Place the chicken wings in a resealable plastic bag or a shallow dish, and coat them with the glaze. Marinate for at least 30 minutes in the refrigerator.

3. Preheat your oven to 375°F (190°C).

4. Line a baking sheet with parchment paper and arrange the marinated chicken wings.

5. Bake the chicken wings in the preheated oven for about 35-40 minutes, or until they are cooked through and the glaze is caramelized.

6. Remove from the oven and let them cool for a few minutes.

7. Garnish with fresh cilantro leaves if desired.

8. Enjoy your apricot-glazed chicken wings as a sweet and savory anti-inflammatory meal.

Per Serving: Calories: 350 Protein: 25g Fat: 20g Salt: 400mg

Sesame-Ginger Turkey Stir-Fry

Total Servings: 1 serving
Preparation Time: 15 minutes
Time to Cook: 10 minutes

Ingredients:

- 4 oz turkey breast, thinly sliced
- 1 tablespoon low-sodium soy sauce
- 1 teaspoon sesame oil
- 1/2 teaspoon minced ginger
- 1/2 teaspoon minced garlic
- 1/2 cup broccoli florets
- 1/2 cup bell pepper strips (any color)
- 1/2 cup snow peas, trimmed
- 1/2 cup sliced carrots
- 1 teaspoon sesame seeds (optional)
- Cooking spray
- Salt and pepper to taste
- Sliced green onions for garnish (optional)

Instructions:

1. Mix the soy sauce, sesame oil, minced ginger, and minced garlic in a small bowl to create a marinade.

2. Place the turkey slices in a resealable plastic bag or a shallow dish, and pour the marinade over them. Seal the bag and shake to coat the turkey. Marinate for at least 30 minutes in the refrigerator.

3. Heat a non-stick skillet or wok over medium-high heat and lightly coat it with cooking spray.

4. Add the marinated turkey slices to the hot skillet and stir-fry for 2-3 minutes until they are no longer pink. Remove from the skillet and set aside.

5. Add broccoli, bell peppers, snow peas, and carrots in the same skillet. Stir-fry for about 5-7 minutes until the vegetables are tender-crisp.

6. Return the cooked turkey to the skillet and toss everything together for another minute to heat through.

7. Transfer the stir-fry to a serving plate and sprinkle with sesame seeds and sliced green onions if desired.

8. Enjoy your sesame-ginger turkey stir-fry as a flavorful and anti-inflammatory meal.

Per Serving: Calories: 35 Protein: 35g Fat: 10g Salt: 600mg

Basil Grilled Quail

Total Servings: 1 serving
Preparation Time: 10 minutes
Time to Cook: 10 minutes

Ingredients:

- 2 quail, split and flattened
- 1 teaspoon olive oil
- 1/2 teaspoon minced garlic
- 1/4 cup fresh basil leaves
- Salt and pepper to taste
- Lemon wedges for serving (optional)

Instructions:

1. Mix the olive oil, minced garlic, salt, and pepper in a small bowl to create a marinade.

2. Place the quail in a resealable plastic bag or a shallow dish, and rub them with the marinade. Marinate for at least 30 minutes in the refrigerator.

3. Preheat your grill to medium-high heat.

4. Grill the quail for about 4-5 minutes per side or until they are cooked through and have grill marks.

5. Remove from the grill and let them rest for a few minutes.

6. Serve with fresh basil leaves and lemon wedges if desired.

7. Enjoy your basil-grilled quail as a delicious and anti-inflammatory meal.

Per Serving: Calories: 280 Protein: 30g Fat: 16g Salt: 400mg

Curry Chicken Drumettes

Total Servings: 1 serving
Preparation Time: 15 minutes

Time to Cook: 20 minutes

Ingredients:
- 4 chicken drumettes (about 4 oz)
- 1 teaspoon olive oil
- 1 teaspoon curry powder
- 1/2 teaspoon minced garlic
- 1/2 teaspoon minced ginger
- Salt and pepper to taste
- Fresh cilantro leaves for garnish (optional)

Instructions:

1. In a small bowl, combine the olive oil, curry powder, minced garlic, ginger, salt, and pepper to create a marinade.

2. Place the chicken drumettes in a resealable plastic bag or a shallow dish, and coat them with the marinade. Marinate for at least 30 minutes in the refrigerator.

3. Preheat your oven to 375°F (190°C).

4. Line a baking sheet with parchment paper and arrange the marinated chicken drumettes.

5. Bake the chicken drumettes in the oven for about 15-20 minutes or until they are cooked and the skin is crispy.

6. Remove from the oven and let them cool for a few minutes.

7. Garnish with fresh cilantro leaves if desired.

8. Enjoy your curry chicken drumettes as a flavorful and anti-inflammatory meal.

Per Serving:
Calories: 320
Protein: 30g
Fat: 20g
Salt: 450mg

Honey Mustard Turkey

Total Servings: 1 serving
Preparation Time: 10 minutes
Time to Cook: 15 minutes

Ingredients:
- 4 oz turkey breast

- 1 tablespoon Dijon mustard
- 1 tablespoon honey
- 1/2 teaspoon olive oil
- 1/2 teaspoon minced garlic
- Salt and pepper to taste
- Fresh parsley for garnish (optional)

Instructions:

1. In a small bowl, combine Dijon mustard, honey, olive oil, minced garlic, salt, and pepper to create a honey mustard marinade.

2. Place the turkey breast in a resealable plastic bag or a shallow dish, and coat it with the marinade. Marinate for at least 30 minutes in the refrigerator.

3. Heat a non-stick skillet over medium-high heat.

4. Add the marinated turkey breast and cook for about 5-7 minutes per side until it is no longer pink in the center and has a golden-brown crust.

5. Remove the turkey breast from the skillet and rest for a few minutes.

6. Slice the turkey and garnish with fresh parsley if desired.

7. Enjoy your honey mustard turkey as a tasty and anti-inflammatory meal.

Per Serving: Calories: 280 Protein: 30g Fat: 8g Salt: 400mg

Paprika Herb Chicken Thighs

Total Servings: 1 serving
Preparation Time: 10 minutes
Time to Cook: 20 minutes

Ingredients:
- 2 bone-in, skinless chicken thighs
- 1 teaspoon olive oil
- 1/2 teaspoon smoked paprika
- 1/2 teaspoon dried thyme
- 1/2 teaspoon dried rosemary
- Salt and pepper to taste
- Fresh thyme sprigs for garnish (optional)

Instructions:

1. Add olive oil, smoked paprika, dried thyme, rosemary, salt, and pepper in a small bowl to create a herb rub.

2. Rub the herb mixture over both sides of the chicken thighs. Marinate for at least 30 minutes in the refrigerator.

3. Preheat your oven to 375°F (190°C).

4. Heat an oven-safe skillet over medium-high heat.

5. Add the marinated chicken thighs and cook for 2-3 minutes per side until they have a golden-brown sear.

6. Transfer the skillet to the preheated oven and bake for approximately 15-18 minutes or until the chicken thighs reach an internal temperature of 165°F (74°C).

7. Remove the chicken from the oven and let it rest for a few minutes.

8. Garnish with fresh thyme sprigs if desired.

9. Enjoy your paprika herb chicken thighs as a flavorful and anti-inflammatory meal.

Per Serving: Calories: 320 Protein: 35g Fat: 18g Salt: 400mg

Spiced Chicken Tenders

Total Servings: 1 serving
Preparation Time: 10 minutes
Time to Cook: 15 minutes

Ingredients:
- 4 chicken tenders (about 4 oz)
- 1 teaspoon olive oil
- 1/2 teaspoon ground cumin
- 1/2 teaspoon paprika
- 1/4 teaspoon cayenne pepper (adjust to your spice preference)
- Salt and pepper to taste
- Fresh cilantro leaves for garnish (optional)

Instructions:

1. Add olive oil, ground cumin, paprika, cayenne pepper, salt, and pepper to create a spice rub in a small bowl.

2. Rub the spice mixture over the chicken tenders. Marinate for at least 30 minutes in the refrigerator.

3. Heat a non-stick skillet over medium-high heat.

4. Add the marinated chicken tenders and cook for about 3-4 minutes per side until they are cooked and have a nice sear.

5. Remove from the skillet and let them rest for a few minutes.

6. Garnish with fresh cilantro leaves if desired.

7. Enjoy your spiced chicken tenders as a delicious and anti-inflammatory meal.

Per Serving: Calories: 280 Protein: 30g Fat: 12g Salt: 450mg

Cranberry-Pecan Turkey

Total Servings: 1 serving
Preparation Time: 10 minutes
Time to Cook: 25 minutes

Ingredients:
- 4 oz turkey breast
- 1/4 cup dried cranberries

- 1/4 cup chopped pecans
- 1/2 teaspoon olive oil
- 1/2 teaspoon dried sage
- Salt and pepper to taste
- Fresh sage leaves for garnish (optional)

Instructions:

1. In a small bowl, combine cranberries, chopped pecans, dried sage, salt, and pepper to create the cranberry-pecan stuffing.

2. Carefully slice a pocket into the side of the turkey breast, creating a space for the stuffing.

3. Stuff the turkey breast with the cranberry-pecan mixture.

4. Rub the outside of the turkey breast with olive oil, salt, and pepper.

5. Preheat your oven to 375°F (190°C).

6. Heat an oven-safe skillet over medium-high heat.

7. Add the turkey breast to the skillet and sear for 2-3 minutes per side until it has a golden-brown crust.

8. Transfer the skillet to the preheated oven and roast for approximately 15-18 minutes or until the turkey reaches an internal temperature of 165°F (74°C).

9. Remove the turkey from the oven and let it rest for a few minute

10. Garnish with fresh sage leaves if desired.

11. Enjoy your cranberry-pecan turkey as a delightful and anti-inflammatory meal.

Per Serving: Calories: 380 Protein: 30g Fat: 18g Salt: 400mg

Pomegranate Glazed Chicken Legs

Total Servings: 1 serving
Preparation Time: 10 minutes
Time to Cook: 30 minutes

Ingredients:
- 2 chicken drumsticks
- 1/4 cup pomegranate juice
- 1 tablespoon honey
- 1/2 teaspoon olive oil
- 1/2 teaspoon minced garlic
- Salt and pepper to taste
- Fresh pomegranate seeds for garnish (optional)

Instructions:

1. To create the glaze, combine pomegranate juice, honey, olive oil, minced garlic, salt, and pepper in a small bowl.

2. Place the chicken drumsticks in a resealable plastic bag or a shallow dish and coat them with the pomegranate glaze. Marinate for at least 30 minutes in the refrigerator.

3. Preheat your oven to 375°F (190°C).

4. Heat an oven-safe skillet over medium-high heat.

5. Add the marinated chicken drumsticks and cook for 2-3 minutes per side until they have a golden-brown sear.

6. Transfer the skillet to the preheated oven and roast for approximately 20-25 minutes or until the chicken legs reach an internal temperature of 165°F (74°C).

7. Remove the chicken from the oven and let it rest for a few minutes.

8. Garnish with fresh pomegranate seeds if desired.

9. Enjoy your pomegranate glazed chicken legs as a flavorful and anti-inflammatory meal.

Per Serving: Calories: 320 Protein: 25g Fat: 10g Salt: 450mg

Herbed Turkey Meatloaf

Total Servings: 1 serving
Preparation Time: 10 minutes
Time to Cook: 30 minutes

Ingredients:
- 4 oz ground turkey
- 1/4 cup rolled oats
- 1/4 cup finely chopped onion
- 1/4 cup grated zucchini
- 1/2 teaspoon dried thyme
- 1/2 teaspoon dried oregano
- Salt and pepper to taste
- Sugar-free ketchup for topping (optional)

Instructions:

1. Preheat your oven to 375°F (190°C).

2. Combine ground turkey, rolled oats, finely chopped onion, grated zucchini, dried thyme, dried oregano, salt, and pepper in a mixing bowl. Mix until all ingredients are well combined.

3. Shape the mixture into a mini meatloaf shape and place it on a baking sheet lined with parchment paper.

4. If desired, spread a thin layer of sugar-free ketchup on top of the meatloaf.

5. Bake in the preheated oven for approximately 25-30 minutes or until the meatloaf is cooked through and has a golden-brown crust.

6. Remove from the oven and let it rest for a few minutes.

7. Slice the meatloaf and serve.

8. Enjoy your herbed turkey meatloaf as a delicious and anti-inflammatory meal.

Per Serving: Calories: 320 Protein: 30g Fat: 10g Salt: 400mg

Lemon-Turmeric Chicken Skewers

Total Servings: 1 serving
Preparation Time: 15 minutes
Time to Cook: 10 minutes

Ingredients:
- 4 oz chicken breast, cut into cubes
- 1/2 lemon, juiced
- 1/2 teaspoon turmeric powder
- 1/2 teaspoon olive oil
- 1/2 teaspoon minced garlic
- Salt and pepper to taste
- Wooden skewers soaked in water

Instructions:

1. In a bowl, combine lemon juice, turmeric powder, olive oil, minced garlic, salt, and pepper to create the marinade.

2. Place the chicken cubes in the marinade and let them marinate in the refrigerator for at least 30 minutes.

3. Preheat your grill or grill pan to medium-high heat.

4. Thread the marinated chicken cubes onto the soaked wooden skewers.

5. Grill the chicken skewers on each side for about 4-5 minutes or until they are cooked through with excellent grill marks.

6. Remove the skewers from the grill and let them rest for a minute.

7. Serve your lemon-turmeric chicken skewers and savor the flavors.

Per Serving: Calories: 220 Protein: 25g Fat: 8g Salt: 300mg

Apricot Sage Turkey Meatballs

Total Servings: 1 serving
Preparation Time: 15 minutes
Time to Cook: 20 minutes

Ingredients:
- 4 oz ground turkey
- 1/4 cup dried apricots, finely chopped
- 1/2 teaspoon dried sage
- 1/2 teaspoon olive oil
- 1/2 teaspoon minced garlic
- Salt and pepper to taste
- Fresh sage leaves for garnish (optional)

Instructions:

1. Combine ground turkey, finely chopped dried apricots, dried sage, olive oil, minced garlic, salt, and pepper in a

mixing bowl. Mix until all ingredients are well combined.

2. Shape the mixture into meatballs.

3. Heat a non-stick skillet over medium heat.

4. Add the turkey meatballs to the skillet and cook for about 10-12 minutes, turning occasionally, until they are cooked and have a golden-brown crust.

5. Remove the meatballs from the skillet and rest for a few minutes.

6. Garnish with fresh sage leaves if desired.

7. Enjoy your apricot sage turkey meatballs as a delightful and anti-inflammatory dish.

Per Serving: Calories: 280 Protein: 24g Fat: 10g Salt: 350mg

Mango Avocado Turkey Salad

Total Servings: 1 serving
Preparation Time: 10 minutes
Time to Assemble: 5 minutes

Ingredients:
- 4 oz cooked turkey breast, diced
- 1/2 ripe mango, diced
- 1/2 ripe avocado, diced
- 1/4 red onion, finely chopped
- 1 tablespoon fresh cilantro, chopped
- 1/2 lime, juiced
- Salt and pepper to taste

Instructions:

1. Combine diced turkey breast, diced mango, avocado, finely chopped red onion, and fresh cilantro in a bowl.

2. Squeeze the juice of half a lime over the salad.

3. Season with salt and pepper to taste.

4. Gently toss all the ingredients together until well-mixed.

5. Serve your mango avocado turkey salad and enjoy the refreshing combination of flavors.

Per Serving: Calories: 320 Protein: 28g Fat: 14g Salt: 400mg

Sesame-Crusted Chicken Tenders

Total Servings: 1 serving
Preparation Time: 15 minutes
Time to Cook: 10 minutes

Ingredients:
- 4 oz chicken tenders
- 1 tablespoon sesame seeds
- 1/2 teaspoon olive oil

- 1/2 teaspoon low-sodium soy sauce
- 1/2 teaspoon minced ginger
- Salt and pepper to taste
- Fresh cilantro for garnish (optional)

Instructions:

1. Combine sesame seeds, olive oil, low-sodium soy sauce, minced ginger, salt, and pepper in a bowl.

2. Coat the chicken tenders with the sesame seed mixture.

3. Heat a non-stick skillet over medium-high heat.

4. Add the sesame-crusted chicken tenders to the skillet and cook for 4-5 minutes on each side or until they are cooked, and the sesame seeds are toasted.

5. Remove the chicken tenders from the skillet and let them rest for a minute.

6. Garnish with fresh cilantro if desired.

7. Enjoy your sesame-crusted chicken tenders as a flavorful and anti-inflammatory meal.

Per Serving: Calories: 290 Protein: 26g Fat: 15g Salt: 420mg

Chapter 5: Fish and Seafood

Lemon-Dill Baked Salmon

Total Servings: 1 serving
Preparation Time: 10 minutes
Time to Cook: 15 minutes

Ingredients:

- 4 oz salmon fillet
- 1/2 lemon, juiced and zested
- 1 teaspoon fresh dill, chopped
- 1/2 teaspoon olive oil
- 1/2 teaspoon minced garlic
- Salt and pepper to taste
- Lemon slices for garnish (optional)

Instructions:

1. In a bowl, combine lemon juice, lemon zest, fresh dill, olive oil, minced garlic, salt, and pepper to create the marinade.

2. Place the salmon fillet in a shallow dish and pour the marinade. Make sure the salmon is coated evenly. Let it marinate in the refrigerator for at least 30 minutes.

3. Preheat your oven to 375°F (190°C).

4. Remove the salmon from the marinade and place it on a baking sheet lined with parchment paper.

5. Bake the salmon in the oven for about 12-15 minutes or until it flakes easily with a fork and has a nice golden color.

6. Remove from the oven and garnish with lemon slices if desired.

7. Serve your lemon-dill baked salmon for a flavorful and anti-inflammatory meal.

Per Serving: Calories: 250 Protein: 25g Fat: 15g Salt: 400mg

Garlic Herb Grilled Shrimp

Total Servings: 1 serving
Preparation Time: 10 minutes)

Time to Cook: 5 minutes

Ingredients:

- 4 oz large shrimp, peeled and deveined
- 1/2 teaspoon olive oil
- 1/2 teaspoon minced garlic
- 1 teaspoon fresh herbs (such as rosemary, thyme, or basil), chopped
- Juice of 1/2 lemon
- Salt and pepper to taste
- Wooden skewers soaked in water

Instructions

1. Add olive oil, minced garlic, fresh herbs, lemon juice, salt, and pepper to create the marinade in a bowl.

2. Add the peeled and deveined shrimp to the marinade, ensuring they are evenly coated. Let them marinate in the refrigerator for about 15-20 minutes.

3. Preheat your grill or grill pan to medium-high heat.

4. Thread the marinated shrimp onto the soaked wooden skewers.

5. Grill the shrimp on each side for 2-3 minutes until they turn pink and have grill marks.

6. Remove the shrimp skewers from the grill.

7. Serve your garlic herb grilled shrimp and enjoy the delicious and anti-inflammatory flavors.

Per Serving: Calories: 160 Protein: 24g Fat: 5g Salt: 300mg

Miso-Glazed Cod Fillets

Total Servings: 1 serving
Preparation Time: 10 minutes
Time to Cook: 12 minutes

Ingredients:

- 4 oz cod fillet
- 1 tablespoon white miso paste
- 1/2 teaspoon honey (or maple syrup for a vegan option)
- 1/2 teaspoon minced ginger
- 1/2 teaspoon sesame oil
- 1/2 teaspoon low-sodium soy sauce (or tamari for a gluten-free option)
- Sesame seeds for garnish (optional)

Instructions:

1. Whisk together white miso paste, honey (or maple syrup), minced ginger, sesame oil, and low-sodium soy sauce to create the miso glaze.

2. Coat the cod fillet with the miso glaze and let it marinate in the refrigerator for at least 30 minutes.

3. Preheat your oven to 375°F (190°C).

4. Place the marinated cod fillet on a baking sheet lined with parchment paper.

5. Bake the cod in the oven for 10-12 minutes or until it flakes easily with a fork and has a beautiful glaze.

6. Remove from the oven and garnish with sesame seeds if desired.

7. Serve your miso-glazed cod fillet as a delicious and anti-inflammatory dish.

Per Serving: Calories: 180 Protein: 22g Fat: 4g Salt: 400mg

Lime Cilantro Grilled Mahi-Mahi

Total Servings: 1 serving
Preparation Time: 10 minutes
Time to Cook: 10 minutes

Ingredients:
- 4 oz Mahi-Mahi fillet
- 1 lime, juiced and zested
- 1 tablespoon fresh cilantro, chopped
- 1/2 teaspoon olive oil
- 1/2 teaspoon minced garlic
- Salt and pepper to taste
- Time wedges for garnish (optional)

Instructions:

1. Combine the lime juice, lime zest, fresh cilantro, olive oil, minced garlic, salt, and pepper to create the marinade.

2. Place the Mahi-Mahi fillet in a shallow dish and pour the marinade. Ensure the fillet is evenly coated. Let it marinate in the refrigerator for at least 30 minutes.

3. Preheat your grill or grill pan to medium-high heat.

4. Remove the Mahi-Mahi from the marinade and grill it for 4-5 minutes on each side or until it s cooked through and has grill marks.

5. Transfer the grilled Mahi-Mahi to a serving plate and garnish with lime wedges if desired.

6. Serve your Lime Cilantro Grilled Mahi-Mahi for a flavorful and anti-inflammatory meal.

Per Serving: Calories: 180 Protein: 30g Fat: 4g Salt: 350mg

Coconut-Curry Tilapia

Total Servings: 1 serving
Preparation Time: 10 minutes
Time to Cook: 15 minutes

Ingredients:
- 4 oz tilapia fillet
- 1/2 cup light coconut milk
- 1 teaspoon curry powder
- 1/2 teaspoon minced ginger
- 1/2 teaspoon minced garlic
- 1/4 cup diced tomatoes
- 1/4 cup diced bell peppers (red, yellow, or green)
- 1/4 cup chopped fresh cilantro

- Salt and pepper to taste
- 1/2 teaspoon coconut oil (for cooking)

Instructions:

1. Combine the light coconut milk, curry powder, minced ginger, and minced garlic in a bowl to create the curry sauce. Set it aside.

2. Heat the coconut oil in a skillet over medium heat.

3. Season the tilapia fillet with salt and pepper, then add it to the skillet. Cook for 2-3 minutes on each side until lightly browned.

4. Remove the tilapia from the skillet and set it aside.

5. In the same skillet, add the diced tomatoes and bell peppers. Sauté for about 2-3 minutes until they start to soften.

6. Pour the curry sauce into the skillet and bring it to a simmer. Cook for an additional 2-3 minutes.

7. Return the tilapia to the skillet, spoon some of the curry sauce over it, and continue to simmer for another 2-3 minutes until the fish is cooked.

8. Garnish with fresh cilantro.

9. Serve your Coconut-Curry Tilapia for a delicious anti-inflammatory meal.

Per Serving: Calories: 250 Protein: 25g Fat: 10g Salt: 400mg

Sesame Tuna Steak

Total Servings: 1 serving
Preparation Time: 10 minutes
Time to Cook: 5 minutes

Ingredients:
- 4 oz tuna steak
- 1 tablespoon low-sodium soy sauce (or tamari for a gluten-free option)
- 1/2 teaspoon sesame oil
- 1/2 teaspoon minced ginger
- 1/2 teaspoon minced garlic
- 1 teaspoon sesame seeds
- Salt and pepper to taste
- Fresh lemon or lime wedges for garnish (optional)

Instructions:

1. Combine the low-sodium soy sauce (or tamari), sesame oil, minced ginger, garlic, sesame seeds, salt, and pepper to create the marinade.

2. Place the tuna steak in a shallow dish and pour the marinade. Ensure the steak is evenly coated. Let it marinate in the refrigerator for at least 30 minutes.

3. Preheat your grill or grill pan to high heat.

4. Remove the tuna steak from the marinade and grill it for 2-3 minutes on each side or until it s seared outside but still pink in the center.

5. Transfer the grilled tuna steak to a serving plate and garnish with fresh lemon or lime wedges if desired.

6. Serve your Sesame Tuna Steak for a flavorful and anti-inflammatory meal.

Per Serving: Calories: 220 Protein: 30g Fat: 8g Salt: 450mg

Paprika Garlic Swordfish

Total Servings: 1 serving
Preparation Time: 10 minutes
Time to Cook: 8-10 minutes

Ingredients:
- 1 swordfish steak (6-8 oz)
- 1 teaspoon paprika
- 1 teaspoon minced garlic
- 1/2 lemon, juiced
- 1/2 teaspoon olive oil
- Salt and pepper to taste
- Fresh parsley for garnish (optional)

Instructions:

1. Combine the paprika, minced garlic, lemon juice, olive oil, salt, and pepper in a bowl to create the marinade.

2. Place the swordfish steak in a shallow dish and pour the marinade. Ensure the steak is evenly coated. Let it marinate in the refrigerator for at least 30 minutes.

3. Preheat your grill or grill pan to medium-high heat.

4. Remove the swordfish from the marinade and grill it for 4-5 minutes on each side or until it›s cooked through and has grill marks.

5. Transfer the grilled swordfish steak to a serving plate and garnish with fresh parsley if desired.

6. Serve your Paprika Garlic Swordfish for a delicious and anti-inflammatory meal.

Per Serving: Calories: 280 Protein: 35g Fat: 13g Salt: 400mg

Citrus-Marinated Grilled Halibut

Total Servings: 1 serving
Preparation Time: 10 minutes
Time to Cook: 8-10 minutes

Ingredients:
- 1 halibut fillet (6-8 oz)
- 1/2 orange, juiced
- 1/2 lemon, juiced
- 1/2 lime, juiced
- 1 teaspoon olive oil
- 1/2 teaspoon minced garlic
- Salt and pepper to taste
- Fresh cilantro for garnish (optional)

Instructions:

1. Combine the orange juice, lemon juice, lime juice, olive oil, minced garlic, salt, and pepper in a bowl to create the citrus marinade.

2. Place the halibut fillet in a shallow dish and pour the marinade. Ensure the fillet is evenly coated. Let it marinate in the refrigerator for at least 30 minutes.

3. Preheat your grill or grill pan to medium-high heat.

4. Remove the halibut from the marinade and grill it for 4-5 minutes on each side or until it s cooked through and has grill marks.

5. Transfer the grilled halibut fillet to a serving plate and garnish with fresh cilantro if desired.

6. Serve your Citrus-Marinated Grilled Halibut for a flavorful and anti-inflammatory meal.

Per Serving: Calories: 240 Protein: 30g Fat: 10g Salt: 380mg

Spicy Sriracha Sardines

Total Servings: 1 serving
Preparation Time: 5 minutes
Time to Cook: 5 minutes

Ingredients:
- 1 can (4 oz) sardines in water, drained
- 1 teaspoon Sriracha sauce (adjust to taste)
- 1/2 teaspoon minced garlic
- 1/2 teaspoon minced ginger
- 1/2 lemon, juiced
- 1/2 teaspoon olive oil
- Salt and pepper to taste
- Fresh cilantro for garnish (optional)

Instructions:

1. Combine the Sriracha sauce, minced garlic, ginger, lemon juice, olive oil, salt, and pepper in a bowl to create the spicy sauce.

2. Heat a non-stick skillet over medium heat and add the drained sardines. Cook for 2-3 minutes on each side until heated through.

3. Pour the spicy sauce over the sardines in the skillet and gently stir to coat them evenly. Cook for an additional 1-2 minutes.

4. Transfer the spicy Sriracha sardines to a serving plate and garnish with fresh cilantro if desired.

5. Serve your Spicy Sriracha Sardines for a zesty and anti-inflammatory meal.

Per Serving: Calories: 210 Protein: 18g Fat: 15g Salt: 420mg

Cajun Blackened Catfish

Total Servings: 1 serving
Preparation Time: 10 minutes
Time to Cook: 10 minutes

Ingredients:
- 1 catfish fillet (6-8 oz)
- 1 teaspoon paprika
- 1/2 teaspoon dried thyme
- 1/2 teaspoon dried oregano
- 1/4 teaspoon cayenne pepper (adjust to taste)
- 1/4 teaspoon garlic powder
- 1/4 teaspoon onion powder
- 1/4 teaspoon salt
- 1/4 teaspoon black pepper
- 1 tablespoon olive oil
- Lemon wedges for garnish (optional)

Instructions:

1. In a small bowl, combine the paprika, dried thyme, oregano, cayenne pepper, garlic powder, onion powder, salt, and black pepper to create the Cajun seasoning.

2. Rub the Cajun seasoning evenly onto both sides of the catfish fillet.

3. Heat the olive oil in a skillet over medium-high heat.

4. Once the oil is hot, add the catfish fillet and cook for 4-5 minutes on each side until it's cooked through and has a blackened crust.

5. Transfer the Cajun Blackened Catfish to a serving plate.

6. Garnish with lemon wedges if desired.

7. Serve your Cajun Blackened Catfish for a spicy and anti-inflammatory meal.

Per Serving: Calories: 280 Protein: 30g Fat: 14g Salt: 600mg

Turmeric Coconut Mussels

Total Servings: 1 serving
Preparation Time: 15 minutes
Time to Cook: 10 minutes

Ingredients:
- 1/2 pound fresh mussels, cleaned and debearded
- 1/2 cup light coconut milk
- 1/2 teaspoon ground turmeric
- 1/2 teaspoon minced garlic
- 1/2 teaspoon minced ginger
- 1/4 teaspoon red pepper flakes (adjust to taste)
- 1/2 tablespoon olive oil
- Fresh cilantro for garnish (optional)
- Lime wedges for garnish (optional)

Instructions:

1. Mix the light coconut milk and ground turmeric in a small bowl to create the turmeric-coconut mixture.

2. Heat the olive oil in a skillet or saucepan over medium heat. Add the minced garlic, minced ginger, and red pepper flakes. Sauté for about 1-2 minutes until fragrant.

3. Add the cleaned mussels to the skillet and stir to coat them with the garlic and ginger.

4. Pour the turmeric-coconut mixture over the mussels. Cover the skillet and let the mussels cook for about 5-7 minutes or until they open up.

5. Discard any unopened mussels.

6. Transfer the Turmeric Coconut Mussels to a serving bowl and garnish with fresh cilantro and lime wedges if desired.

7. Serve your Turmeric Coconut Mussels for a flavorful and anti-inflammatory meal.

Per Serving: Calories: 250 Protein: 20g Fat: 15g Salt: 450mg

Baked Teriyaki Salmon

Total Servings: 1 serving
Preparation Time: 10 minutes
Time to Cook: 15 minutes

Ingredients:
- 1 salmon fillet (6-8 oz)
- 2 tablespoons reduced-sodium soy sauce
- 1 tablespoon honey
- 1/2 teaspoon minced garlic
- 1/2 teaspoon minced ginger
- 1/2 teaspoon sesame seeds (optional)
- Sliced green onions for garnish (optional)

Instructions:

1. Mix the reduced-sodium soy sauce, honey, minced garlic, and ginger to create the teriyaki marinade in a bowl.

2. Place the salmon fillet in a shallow dish and pour the teriyaki marinade. Ensure the fillet is evenly coated. Let it marinate in the refrigerator for at least 30 minutes.

3. Preheat your oven to 375°F (190°C).

4. Place the marinated salmon fillet on a baking sheet lined with parchment paper. Sprinkle sesame seeds on top if desired.

5. Bake the salmon for about 12-15 minutes or until it flakes easily with a fork and has a caramelized glaze.

6. Transfer the Baked Teriyaki Salmon to a serving plate and garnish with sliced green onions if desired.

7. Serve your Baked Teriyaki Salmon for a sweet and savory anti-inflammatory meal.

Per Serving: Calories: 320 Protein: 30g Fat: 14g
Salt: 700mg

Lemon Garlic Sea Bass

Total Servings: 1 serving
Preparation Time: 10 minutes
Time to Cook: 15 minutes

Ingredients:

- 1 sea bass fillet (6-8 oz)
- 1 lemon, juiced and zested
- 2 cloves garlic, minced
- 1 tablespoon olive oil
- 1/2 teaspoon dried oregano
- Salt and pepper to taste
- Fresh parsley for garnish (optional)
- Lemon wedges for garnish (optional)

Instructions:

1. Combine the lemon juice, lemon zest, minced garlic, olive oil, dried oregano, salt, and pepper in a small bowl. This creates the lemon garlic marinade.

2. Place the sea bass fillet in a shallow dish and pour the lemon garlic marinade. Ensure the fillet is evenly coated. Let it marinate in the refrigerator for at least 30 minutes.

3. Preheat your oven to 375°F (190°C).

4. Heat an ovenproof skillet over medium-high heat. Add a bit of olive oil.

5. Once the skillet is hot, place the marinated sea bass fillet skin-side down into the skillet. Sear for 2-3 minutes until the skin becomes crispy and golden.

6. Transfer the skillet to the preheated oven and bake for 10-12 minutes or until the sea bass is cooked and flakes easily with a fork.

7. Garnish your Lemon Garlic Sea Bass with fresh parsley and lemon wedges if desired.

8. Serve your Lemon Garlic Sea Bass for a flavorful and anti-inflammatory meal.

Per Serving: Calories: 280 Protein: 30g Fat: 15g
Salt: 400mg

Chili Lime Shrimp Tacos

Total Servings: 1 serving
Preparation Time: 15 minutes
Time to Cook: 10 minutes

Ingredients:

- 6-8 large shrimp, peeled and deveined
- 1 lime, juiced and zested
- 1 clove garlic, minced
- 1/2 teaspoon chili powder
- 1/4 teaspoon cumin
- Salt and pepper to taste
- 2 small corn tortillas
- 1/4 cup shredded red cabbage
- 1/4 avocado, sliced
- Fresh cilantro for garnish (optional)
- Sliced radishes for garnish (optional)

Instructions:

1. Combine the lime juice, lime zest, minced garlic, chili powder, cumin, salt, and pepper to create the marinade.

2. Place the shrimp in a shallow dish and pour the marinade over them. Ensure the shrimp are evenly coated. Let them marinate in the refrigerator for about 15 minutes.

3. Heat a skillet over medium-high heat. Add a bit of olive oil.

4. Once the skillet is hot, add the marinated shrimp and cook for 2-3 minutes on each side until they turn pink and opaque.

5. Warm the corn tortillas in the skillet for a minute on each side.

6. Assemble your Chili Lime Shrimp Tacos: Place the cooked shrimp on the warm tortillas and top with shredded red cabbage, sliced avocado, fresh cilantro, and sliced radishes if desired.

7. Serve your Chili Lime Shrimp Tacos for a zesty and anti-inflammatory meal.

Per Serving: Calories: 300 Protein: 20g Fat: 10g
Salt: 450mg

Orange Glazed Scallops

Total Servings: 1 serving
Preparation Time: 10 minutes
Time to Cook: 10 minutes

Ingredients:

- 4 large scallops
- 1 orange, juiced and zested
- 1 tablespoon honey
- 1/2 teaspoon grated ginger
- 1/4 teaspoon red pepper flakes (adjust to taste)
- Salt and pepper to taste
- 1/2 tablespoon olive oil
- Fresh chives for garnish (optional)
- Orange wedges for garnish (optional)

Instructions:

1. Combine the orange juice, orange zest, honey, grated ginger, red pepper flakes, salt, and pepper to create the orange glaze in a bowl.

2. Place the scallops in a shallow dish and pour the orange glaze over them. Ensure the scallops are evenly coated. Let them marinate in the refrigerator for about 15 minutes.

3. Heat a skillet over medium-high heat. Add the olive oil.

4. Once the skillet is hot, add the marinated scallops and cook for 2-3 minutes on each side until they turn golden brown and have a caramelized glaze.

5. Transfer the Orange Glazed Scallops to a serving plate and garnish with fresh chives and orange wedges if desired.

6. Serve your Orange Glazed Scallops for a sweet and tangy anti-inflammatory meal.

Per Serving: Calories: 220 Protein: 15g Fat: 5g Salt: 350mg

Lemon Herb Poached Cod

Total Servings: 1 serving
Preparation Time: 10 minutes
Time to Cook: 10 minutes

Ingredients:
- 1 cod fillet (6-8 oz)
- 1 lemon, thinly sliced
- 2 sprigs fresh thyme
- 1 clove garlic, minced
- 1 cup vegetable broth
- Salt and pepper to taste
- Fresh parsley for garnish (optional)

Instructions:

1. Combine the vegetable broth, lemon slices, fresh thyme sprigs, minced garlic, salt, and pepper in a shallow pan or skillet. This creates the poaching liquid.

2. Heat the poaching liquid over medium-high heat until it simmers gently.

3. Carefully place the cod fillet into the simmering liquid.

4. Cover the pan and poach the cod for about 5-7 minutes until it becomes opaque and flakes easily with a fork.

5. Remove the poached cod from the liquid and place it on a serving plate.

6. Garnish your Lemon Herb Poached Cod with fresh parsley if desired.

7. Serve your Lemon Herb Poached Cod for a light and anti-inflammatory meal.

Per Serving: Calories: 180 Protein: 30g Fat: 4g Salt: 550mg

Cilantro-Lime Octopus

Total Servings: 1 serving
Preparation Time: 15 minutes
Time to Cook: 10 minutes

Ingredients:
- 1 octopus tentacle (6-8 oz)
- 1 lime, juiced and zested
- 2 tablespoons fresh cilantro, chopped
- 1 clove garlic, minced
- 1/4 teaspoon red pepper flakes (adjust to taste)
- Salt and pepper to taste
- 1/2 tablespoon olive oil
- Lime wedges for garnish (optional)

Instructions:

1. Combine the lime juice, lime zest, chopped cilantro, minced garlic, red pepper flakes, salt, and pepper in a bowl. This creates the marinade.

2. Place the octopus tentacle in a shallow dish and pour the marinade over it. Ensure the octopus is evenly coated. Let it marinate in the refrigerator for about 15 minutes.

3. Heat a skillet over medium-high heat. Add the olive oil.

4. Once the skillet is hot, add the marinated octopus tentacle and cook for 2-3 minutes on each side until it turns golden brown and slightly crispy.

5. Transfer the Cilantro-Lime Octopus to a serving plate and garnish with lime wedges if desired.

6. Serve your Cilantro-Lime Octopus for a zesty and anti-inflammatory meal.

Per Serving: Calories: 200 Protein: 20g Fat: 7g Salt: 450mg

Herbed Lobster Tails

Total Servings: 1 serving
Preparation Time: 10 minutes
Time to Cook: 10 minutes

Ingredients:
- 1 lobster tail (6-8 oz)
- 2 tablespoons fresh herbs (such as parsley, basil, and thyme), chopped
- 1 clove garlic, minced
- 1/2 tablespoon olive oil
- Lemon wedges for garnish (optional)
- Salt and pepper to taste

Instructions:

1. Preheat your broiler or grill to medium-high heat.

2. Combine the chopped fresh herbs, minced garlic, olive oil, salt, and pepper in a small bowl. This creates the herbed marinade.

3. Using kitchen shears, carefully cut the top shell of the lobster tail down the center. Spread the body slightly to expose the lobster meat.

4. Brush the lobster meat with the herbed marinade, ensuring it›s evenly coated.

5. Place the lobster tail on the preheated grill or under the broiler. Cook for 5-7 minutes or until the lobster meat is opaque and slightly caramelized.

6. Transfer the Herbed Lobster Tail to a serving plate and garnish with lemon wedges if desired.

7. Serve your Herbed Lobster Tail for an indulgent and anti-inflammatory meal.

Per Serving: Calories: 150 Protein: 20g Fat: 7g Salt: 350mg

Garlic Herb Haddock

Total Servings: 1 serving
Preparation Time: 10 minutes
Time to Cook: 10 minutes

Ingredients:
- 1 haddock fillet (6-8 oz)
- 2 cloves garlic, minced
- 1 tablespoon fresh herbs (such as parsley, thyme, and rosemary), chopped
- 1/2 tablespoon olive oil
- Juice of 1/2 lemon
- Salt and pepper to taste
- Lemon wedges for garnish (optional)

Instructions:

1. Preheat your oven to 375°F (190°C).

2. Combine the minced garlic, chopped fresh herbs, olive oil, lemon juice, salt, and pepper in a small bowl. This creates the garlic herb marinade.

3. Place the haddock fillet on a baking sheet lined with parchment paper.

4. Brush the haddock fillet with the garlic herb marinade, ensuring it›s evenly coated.

5. Bake the haddock in the oven for about 10 minutes, or until the fish flakes easily with a fork and the top is slightly golden.

6. Transfer the Garlic Herb Haddock to a serving plate and garnish with lemon wedges if desired.

7. Serve your Garlic Herb Haddock for a flavorful and anti-inflammatory meal.

Per Serving: Calories: 180 Protein: 20g Fat: 6g Salt: 400mg

Sesame Wasabi Tuna

Total Servings: 1 serving
Preparation Time: 10 minutes
Time to Cook: 5 minutes

Ingredients:
- 1 tuna steak (6-8 oz)
- 1 tablespoon sesame oil
- 1 tablespoon low-sodium soy sauce (or tamari for a gluten-free option)
- 1/2 teaspoon wasabi paste (adjust to taste)

- 1/2 teaspoon honey (or maple syrup for a vegan option)
- Sesame seeds for garnish (optional)
- Salt and pepper to taste

Instructions:

1. Whisk together the sesame oil, low-sodium soy sauce, wasabi paste, honey, salt, and pepper in a bowl. This creates the sesame wasabi marinade.

2. Place the tuna steak in a shallow dish and pour the marinade. Ensure the tuna is evenly coated. Let it marinate in the refrigerator for about 10-15 minutes.

3. Heat a skillet or grill pan over medium-high heat.

4. Once hot, add the marinated tuna steak and cook for 2-3 minutes on each side or until the tuna is seared outside and still slightly pink in the center.

5. Transfer the Sesame Wasabi Tuna to a serving plate and sprinkle with sesame seeds if desired.

6. Serve your Sesame Wasabi Tuna for a zesty and anti-inflammatory meal.

Per Serving: Calories: 250 Protein: 30g Fat: 12g Salt: 500mg

Citrus-Marinated Shrimp Skewers

Total Servings: 1 serving
Preparation Time: 15 minutes
Time to Cook: 5 minutes

Ingredients:
- 8 large shrimp, peeled and deveined
- Zest and juice of 1/2 orange
- Zest and juice of 1/2 lemon
- 1 tablespoon fresh herbs (such as cilantro and mint), chopped
- 1/2 tablespoon olive oil
- Salt and pepper to taste
- Wooden skewer, soaked in water (for grilling)

Instructions:

1. Combine the orange zest, lemon zest, orange juice, lemon juice, chopped fresh herbs, olive oil, salt, and pepper in a bowl. This creates the citrus marinade.

2. Thread the marinated shrimp onto the soaked wooden skewer.

3. Place the shrimp skewer on a preheated grill or pan over medium-high heat.

4. Grill the shrimp on each side for 2-3 minutes until they turn pink and slightly caramelized.

5. Transfer the Citrus-Marinated Shrimp Skewers to a serving plate.

6. Serve your Citrus-Marinated Shrimp Skewers for a refreshing and anti-inflammatory meal.

Per Serving: Calories: 120 Protein: 20g Fat: 4g
Salt: 350mg

Cucumber Marinated Salmon

Total Servings: 1 serving
Preparation Time: 15 minutes
Time to Cook: 10 minutes

Ingredients:
- 1 salmon fillet (6-8 oz)
- 1/2 cucumber, thinly sliced
- 1/4 cup fresh dill, chopped
- 2 tablespoons white wine vinegar
- 1 tablespoon olive oil
- 1/2 teaspoon honey (or maple syrup for a vegan option)
- Salt and pepper to taste
- Lemon wedges for garnish (optional)

Instructions:

1. Combine the white wine vinegar, olive oil, honey, salt, and pepper in a bowl. This creates the cucumber marinade.

2. Place the thinly sliced cucumber and chopped fresh dill into the marinade. Toss to coat, and let it marinate in the refrigerator for 10-15 minutes.

3. Season the salmon fillet with a pinch of salt and pepper.

4. Heat a skillet over medium-high heat.

5. Once hot, add the salmon fillet and cook for 4-5 minutes on each side or until the salmon is cooked to your desired level of doneness.

6. Place the marinated cucumber and dill mixture on a serving plate and top with the cooked salmon.

7. Garnish with lemon wedges if desired.

8. Serve your Cucumber Marinated Salmon for a refreshing and anti-inflammatory meal.

Per Serving: Calories: 350 Protein: 30g Fat: 20g
Salt: 300mg

Cajun Crawfish Boil

Total Servings: 1 serving
Preparation Time: 15 minutes
Time to Cook: 20 minutes

Ingredients:
- 1 cup crawfish tails (pre-cooked and peeled)
- 1 small corn on the cob, cut into chunks
- 6 small red potatoes
- 1/2 teaspoon Cajun seasoning (adjust to taste)
- 1/2 teaspoon paprika
- 1/4 teaspoon garlic powder
- 1/4 teaspoon onion powder

- 1/4 teaspoon dried thyme
- 1/4 teaspoon dried oregano
- Salt to taste
- Lemon wedges for garnish (optional)

Instructions:

1. In a large pot, bring water to a boil. Add the red potatoes and cook for 10-12 minutes or until they're almost tender.

2. Add the corn chunks to the pot and continue boiling for 5 minutes.

3. Drain the water from the pot, leaving the potatoes and corn.

4. Season the potatoes and corn with Cajun seasoning, paprika, garlic powder, onion powder, dried thyme, dried oregano, and salt. Toss to coat evenly.

5. Add the pre-cooked and peeled crawfish tails to the pot and gently stir everything together.

6. Cover the pot and cook on low heat for about 5-7 minutes or until the crawfish tails are heated.

7. Transfer the Cajun Crawfish Boil to a serving plate.

8. Garnish with lemon wedges if desired.

9. Serve your Cajun Crawfish Boil for a spicy and anti-inflammatory meal.

Per Serving: Calories: 300 Protein: 20g Fat: 1g
Salt: 400mg

Blackened Snapper Mango

Total Servings: 1 serving
Preparation Time: 10 minutes
Time to Cook: 8 minutes

Ingredients:
- 1 snapper fillet (6-8 oz)
- 1/2 teaspoon paprika
- 1/2 teaspoon onion powder
- 1/2 teaspoon garlic powder
- 1/4 teaspoon cayenne pepper (adjust to taste)
- 1/4 teaspoon dried thyme
- 1/4 teaspoon dried oregano
- 1/4 teaspoon black pepper
- Salt to taste
- 1/2 ripe mango, peeled and diced
- 1/4 red onion, finely chopped
- 1 tablespoon fresh cilantro, chopped
- Juice of 1/2 lime
- Lime wedges for garnish (optional)

Instructions:

1. Combine paprika, onion powder, garlic powder, cayenne pepper, dried thyme, dried oregano, black pepper, and salt in a small bowl. This creates the blackening seasoning.

2. Season both sides of the snapper fillet with the blackening seasoning.

3. Heat a skillet over medium-high heat.

4. Once hot, add the snapper fillet and cook for about 4 minutes on each side or until the snapper is blackened and cooked through.

5. Combine diced mango, finely chopped red onion, fresh cilantro, and lime juice in a separate bowl. Toss to combine.

6. Transfer the Blackened Snapper to a serving plate and top with the mango salsa.

7. Garnish with lime wedges if desired.

8. Serve your Blackened Snapper Mango for a zesty and anti-inflammatory meal.

Per Serving: Calories: 300 Protein: 30g Fat: 5g Salt: 500mg

Lemon-Garlic Crab Legs

Total Servings: 1 serving
Preparation Time: 10 minutes
Time to Cook: 5 minutes

Ingredients:
- 1 cluster of crab legs (6-8 oz)
- 1 lemon, sliced
- 2 cloves garlic, minced
- 1 tablespoon olive oil
- Salt and pepper to taste
- Fresh parsley for garnish (optional)

Instructions:

1. Preheat your grill to medium-high heat.

2. Mix minced garlic, olive oil, salt, and pepper in a small bowl.

3. Lay a large sheet of aluminum foil on a flat surface. Place the crab legs on the foil.

4. Drizzle the garlic and olive oil mixture over the crab legs.

5. Lay lemon slices on top of the crab legs.

6. Carefully fold the aluminum foil around the crab legs, creating a sealed packet.

7. Place the foil packet on the preheated grill.

8. Grill for about 5 minutes or until the crab legs are heated through.

9. Open the foil packet and transfer the crab legs to a serving plate

10. Garnish with fresh parsley if desired.

11. Serve your Lemon-Garlic Crab Legs for a flavorful and anti-inflammatory meal.

Per Serving: Calories: 250 Protein: 20g Fat: 12g Salt: 600mg

Turmeric Coconut Shrimp

Total Servings: 1 serving
Preparation Time: 10 minutes
Time to Cook: 10 minutes

Ingredients:
- 6-8 large shrimp, peeled and deveined
- 1/2 cup light coconut milk
- 1/2 teaspoon turmeric powder
- 1/2 teaspoon curry powder
- 1/4 teaspoon garlic powder
- 1/4 teaspoon ginger powder
- Salt and pepper to taste
- 1/4 cup fresh cilantro, chopped
- 1/4 lime, juiced
- Lime wedges for garnish (optional)

Instructions:

1. Combine coconut milk, turmeric powder, curry powder, garlic powder, ginger powder, salt, and pepper in a bowl. This creates the marinade.

2. Place the shrimp in the marinade and toss to coat. Let it marinate for about 10 minutes.

3. Heat a skillet over medium-high heat.

4. Once hot, add the marinated shrimp and cook for about 2-3 minutes on each side until the shrimp turn pink and are cooked through.

5. In a separate bowl, combine fresh cilantro and lime juice.

6. Transfer the cooked Turmeric Coconut Shrimp to a serving plate and garnish with cilantro-lime mixture.

7. Serve your Turmeric Coconut Shrimp for a fragrant and anti-inflammatory meal.

Per Serving: Calories: 250 Protein: 20g Fat: 10g Salt: 450mg

Mango Avocado Tuna Salad

Total Servings: 1 serving
Preparation Time: 10 minutes
Time to Assemble: 5 minutes

Ingredients:
- 1 can (5 oz) tuna in water, drained
- 1/2 ripe avocado, diced
- 1/2 ripe mango, diced
- 1/4 red onion, finely chopped
- 1/4 cup cucumber, diced
- 1/4 cup cherry tomatoes, halved
- 1 tablespoon fresh cilantro, chopped

- 1 tablespoon extra-virgin olive oil
- Juice of 1/2 lime
- Salt and pepper to taste
- Fresh basil leaves for garnish (optional)

Instructions:

1. Combine diced avocado, diced mango, finely chopped red onion, diced cucumber, halved cherry tomatoes, and chopped fresh cilantro in a bowl.

2. In a separate bowl, flake the drained tuna.

3. Add the flaked tuna to the bowl of mixed fruits and vegetables.

4. Drizzle extra-virgin olive oil and lime juice over the salad.

5. Season with salt and pepper, and gently toss to combine all ingredients.

6. Transfer the Mango Avocado Tuna Salad to a serving plate.

7. Garnish with fresh basil leaves if desired.

8. Serve your Mango Avocado Tuna Salad for a refreshing and anti-inflammatory meal.

Per Serving: Calories: 350 Protein: 20g Fat: 20g Salt: 300mg

Ginger Soy Sea Bass

Total Servings: 1 serving
Preparation Time: 10 minutes
Time to Cook: 15 minutes

Ingredients:

- 1 sea bass fillet (6-8 oz)
- 1 tablespoon low-sodium soy sauce
- 1 teaspoon fresh ginger, minced
- 1 clove garlic, minced
- 1/2 teaspoon sesame oil
- 1/4 teaspoon honey
- 1/4 teaspoon black pepper
- 1/4 teaspoon red pepper flakes (optional)
- Sliced green onions for garnish (optional)

Instructions:

1. Preheat your oven to 375°F (190°C).

2. In a small bowl, whisk together soy sauce, ginger, garlic, sesame oil, honey, black pepper, and red pepper flakes (if using). This creates the ginger soy marinade.

3. Place the sea bass fillet on a baking sheet lined with parchment paper.

4. Pour the ginger soy marinade over the sea bass, ensuring it›s evenly coated.

5. Bake the sea bass in the oven for about 12-15 minutes or until it flakes easily with a fork and is cooked through.

6. Transfer the cooked Ginger Soy Sea Bass to a serving plate.

7. Garnish with sliced green onions if desired.

8. Serve your Ginger Soy Sea Bass for a flavorful and anti-inflammatory meal.

Per Serving: Calories: 250 Protein: 30g Fat: 10g Salt: 450mg

Mediterranean Sardines

Total Servings: 1 serving
Preparation Time: 10 minutes
Time to Cook: 10 minutes

Ingredients:

- 4-6 fresh sardines, gutted and cleaned
- 1 tablespoon olive oil
- 2 cloves garlic, minced
- 1 teaspoon dried oregano
- 1/2 lemon, sliced
- Salt and pepper to taste
- Fresh parsley for garnish (optional)

Instructions:

1. Preheat your grill to medium-high heat.

2. Add olive oil, minced garlic, dried oregano, salt, and pepper in a small bowl. This creates the Mediterranean marinade.

3. Brush the marinade over the sardines, ensuring they are well coated.

4. Place the sardines on the preheated grill and grill for about 4-5 minutes on each side or until they are cooked through and have grill marks.

5. Transfer the grilled Mediterranean Sardines to a serving plate.

6. Garnish with lemon slices and fresh parsley if desired.

7. Serve your Mediterranean Sardines for a delicious and anti-inflammatory meal.

Per Serving: Calories: 300 Protein: 25g Fat: 20g Salt: 350mg

Lemon-Herb Baked Trout

Total Servings: 1 serving
Preparation Time: 10 minutes
Time to Cook: 20 minutes

Ingredients:

- 1 trout fillet (6-8 oz)
- 1/2 lemon, thinly sliced
- 1 sprig of fresh rosemary
- 1 sprig of fresh thyme
- 1 clove garlic, minced
- 1 tablespoon olive oil

- Salt and pepper to taste
- Fresh parsley for garnish (optional)

Instructions:

1. Preheat your oven to 375°F (190°C).

2. Place the trout fillet on a baking sheet lined with parchment paper.

3. Combine minced garlic, olive oil, salt, and pepper in a small bowl. Brush this mixture over the trout fillet.

4. Lay lemon slices on top of the trout fillet.

5. Place the fresh rosemary and thyme sprigs on the trout.

6. Bake in the preheated oven for about 18-20 minutes or until the trout flakes easily with a fork and is cooked through.

7. Transfer the cooked Lemon-Herb Baked Trout to a serving plate.

8. Garnish with fresh parsley if desired.

9. Serve your Lemon-Herb Baked Trout for a zesty and anti-inflammatory meal.

Per Serving: Calories: 280 Protein: 30g Fat: 16g Salt: 400mg

Chapter 6: Vegetarian and Vegan

Turmeric Lentil Soup

Total Servings: 1 serving
Preparation Time: 10 minutes
Time to Cook: 25 minutes

Ingredients:

- 1/2 cup red lentils
- 1 1/2 cups vegetable broth
- 1/2 cup diced carrots
- 1/2 cup diced celery
- 1/2 cup diced onion
- 1 clove garlic, minced
- 1/2 teaspoon ground turmeric
- 1/2 teaspoon ground cumin
- Salt and pepper to taste
- Fresh cilantro for garnish (optional)

Instructions:

1. Rinse the red lentils thoroughly under cold water and drain.

2. Heat a tablespoon of olive oil over medium heat in a medium-sized pot. Add the diced onions, carrots, and celery. Sauté for about 5 minutes until the vegetables begin to soften.

3. Add the minced garlic, turmeric, and ground cumin to the pot. Sauté for another 1-2 minutes until fragrant.

4. Pour in the vegetable broth and add the rinsed red lentils. Bring the mixture to a boil.

5. Reduce the heat, cover, and let the soup simmer for about 20-25 minutes or until the lentils and vegetables are tender.

6. Season with salt and pepper to taste.

7. Ladle the Turmeric Lentil Soup into a bowl.

8. Garnish with fresh cilantro if desired.

9. Serve your Turmeric Lentil Soup for a comforting and anti-inflammatory meal.

Per Serving: Calories: 300 Protein: 18g Fat: 2g Salt: 600mg

Roasted Veggie Quinoa Salad

Total Servings: 1 serving
Preparation Time: 15 minutes
Time to Cook: 20 minutes

Ingredients:

- 1/2 cup quinoa
- 1 cup water or vegetable broth
- 1 cup mixed roasted vegetables (e.g., bell peppers, zucchini, cherry tomatoes)
- 1/4 cup chopped fresh spinach
- 1/4 cup diced cucumber
- 1/4 cup diced red onion
- 1 tablespoon extra-virgin olive oil
- 1 tablespoon balsamic vinegar
- Salt and pepper to taste
- Fresh basil leaves for garnish (optional)

Instructions:

1. Rinse the quinoa under cold water and drain.

2. In a small saucepan, combine the quinoa and water or vegetable broth. Bring to a boil, then reduce the heat to low, cover, and simmer for 15-20 minutes or until the liquid is absorbed and the quinoa is fluffy.

3. Combine the cooked quinoa, roasted vegetables, chopped spinach, diced cucumber, and red onion in a large bowl.

4. Whisk together the extra-virgin olive oil and balsamic vinegar in a small bowl to create the dressing.

5. Drizzle the dressing over the salad and toss to combine. Season with salt and pepper to taste.

6. Garnish with fresh basil leaves if desired.

7. Serve your Roasted Veggie Quinoa Salad for a nutritious and anti-inflammatory meal.

Per Serving: Calories: 350 Protein: 8g Fat: 10g Salt: 300mg

Mango Avocado Spinach Salad

Total Servings: 1 serving
Preparation Time: 10 minutes
Time to Serve: 0 minutes (no cooking required)

Ingredients:

- 2 cups fresh spinach leaves
- 1/2 ripe mango, diced
- 1/2 ripe avocado, diced
- 1/4 cup red onion, thinly sliced
- 1 tablespoon extra-virgin olive oil
- 1 tablespoon balsamic vinegar
- Salt and pepper to taste
- Toasted almonds for garnish (optional)

Instructions:

1. Combine the fresh spinach leaves, diced mango, avocado, and thinly sliced red onion in a large bowl.

2. Whisk together the extra-virgin olive oil and balsamic vinegar in a small bowl to create the dressing.

3. Drizzle the dressing over the salad and toss to combine. Season with salt and pepper to taste.

4. Garnish with toasted almonds if desired.

5. Serve your Mango Avocado Spinach Salad for a refreshing and anti-inflammatory meal.

Per Serving: Calories: 350 Protein: 4g Fat: 16g
Salt: 400mg

Vegan Chickpea Curry

Total Servings: 1 serving
Preparation Time: 15 minutes
Time to Cook: 25 minutes

Ingredients:
- 1/2 cup canned chickpeas, drained and rinsed
- 1/2 cup diced tomatoes (canned or fresh)
- 1/4 cup diced onion
- 1/4 cup diced bell pepper (any color)
- 1/4 cup diced zucchini
- 1/4 cup coconut milk
- 1 tsp olive oil
- 1 tsp curry powder
- 1/2 tsp ground cumin
- 1/2 tsp ground coriander
- 1/4 tsp turmeric
- 1/4 tsp paprika
- Salt and pepper to taste
- Fresh cilantro leaves for garnish

Instructions:

1. Heat the olive oil in a non-stick pan over medium heat.

2. Add diced onions, bell pepper, and zucchini. Sauté for about 3-4 minutes until they start to soften.

3. Add the curry powder, cumin, coriander, turmeric, and paprika. Cook for another 2 minutes to toast the spices, stirring constantly.

4. Stir in the diced tomatoes and chickpeas. Cook for 5 minutes, allowing the flavors to meld and the tomatoes to soften.

5. Pour in the coconut milk and mix well. Simmer for an additional 10 minutes, allowing the curry to thicken slightly.

6. Season with salt and pepper to taste.

7. Serve hot, garnished with fresh cilantro leaves.

Per serving: Calories: 350 Protein: 9g Fat: 15g
Salt: 600mg

Stuffed Quinoa Bell Peppers

Total Servings: 1 serving
Preparation Time: 15 minutes
Time to Cook: 40 minutes

Ingredients:
- 1 large bell pepper, any color
- 1/2 cup cooked quinoa
- 1/4 cup black beans, drained and rinsed
- 1/4 cup corn kernels
- 1/4 cup diced tomatoes
- 1/4 cup diced red onion
- 1/4 cup diced avocado
- 1/4 tsp chili powder
- 1/4 tsp cumin
- Salt and pepper to taste
- Fresh cilantro leaves for garnish

Instructions:

1. Preheat the oven to 375°F (190°C).

2. Cut the top off the bell pepper and remove the seeds and membranes. Set aside.

3. Combine the cooked quinoa, black beans, corn, diced tomatoes, red onion, and avocado in a bowl.

4. Season the mixture with chili powder, cumin, salt, and pepper. Mix well.

5. Stuff the bell pepper with the quinoa mixture, gently pressing it down to pack it.

6. Place the stuffed pepper in a baking dish and cover with aluminum foil.

7. Bake for 30-35 minutes or until the pepper is tender.

8. Garnish with fresh cilantro leaves before serving.

Per serving: Calories: 400 Protein: 12g Fat: 10g
Salt: 350mg

Creamy Sweet Potato Soup

Total Servings: 1 serving
Preparation Time: 15 minutes
Time to Cook: 30 minutes

Ingredients:
- 1 small sweet potato, peeled and diced
- 1/4 cup diced onion
- 1/4 cup diced celery
- 1/4 cup diced carrots
- 1/4 cup canned coconut milk
- 1 cup vegetable broth
- 1/2 tsp olive oil
- 1/4 tsp ground ginger
- 1/4 tsp ground cinnamon
- Salt and pepper to taste
- Chopped fresh chives for garnish

Instructions:

1. In a pot, heat the olive oil over medium heat.

2. Add the diced onion, celery, and carrots. Sauté for about 5 minutes until they start to soften.

3. Stir in the diced sweet potato, ginger, cinnamon, salt, and pepper. Cook for another 2-3 minutes, making the spices fragrant.

4. Pour in the vegetable broth and bring to a boil. Reduce heat, cover, and simmer for 20-25 minutes until the sweet potatoes are tender.

5. Remove from heat and let it cool slightly.

6. Use an immersion blender to blend the soup until smooth and creamy.

7. Stir in the canned coconut milk and heat gently without boiling.

8. Serve hot, garnished with chopped fresh chives.

Per serving: Calories: 350 Protein: 4g Fat: 15g Salt: 500mg

Spaghetti Squash with Tomato Sauce

Total Servings: 1 serving
Preparation Time: 15 minutes
Time to Cook: 45 minutes

Ingredients:
- 1 small spaghetti squash
- 1 cup diced tomatoes (canned or fresh)
- 1/4 cup diced onion
- 1/4 cup diced bell pepper
- 1 clove garlic, minced
- 1 teaspoon olive oil
- 1/2 teaspoon dried basil
- 1/2 teaspoon dried oregano
- Salt and pepper to taste

Instructions:

1. Preheat your oven to 375°F (190°C).

2. Carefully cut the spaghetti squash in half lengthwise and scoop the seeds with a spoon. Place the halves, cut side up, on a baking sheet.

3. Roast the spaghetti squash in the preheated oven for about 35-40 minutes or until the flesh is tender and can easily be scraped with a fork to create spaghetti-like strands. Remove from the oven and let it cool slightly.

4. While the squash is roasting, prepare the tomato sauce. Heat the olive oil in a saucepan over medium heat. Add the diced onion, bell pepper, and garlic. Sauté for 2-3 minutes until they begin to soften.

5. Add the diced tomatoes, dried basil, oregano, salt, and pepper to the saucepan. Stir well and let it simmer for 10-15 minutes, allowing the flavors to meld together. You can add a splash of water if the sauce becomes too thick.

6. Once the spaghetti squash is done roasting, use a fork to

scrape the flesh into strands. Transfer the spaghetti squash to a plate.

7. Pour the tomato sauce over the spaghetti squash, garnish with fresh basil if desired, and serve hot.

Per Serving: Calories: 200 Protein: 3g Fat: 4g Salt: 300mg

Cauliflower Chickpea Bowl

Total Servings: 1 serving
Preparation Time: 15 minutes
Time to Cook: 25 minutes

Ingredients:
- 1 cup cauliflower florets
- 1/2 cup chickpeas, cooked
- 1/2 cup broccoli florets
- 1/4 cup diced red onion
- 1 clove garlic, minced
- 1 teaspoon olive oil
- 1/2 teaspoon ground cumin
- 1/2 teaspoon ground turmeric
- Salt and pepper to taste
- Juice of half a lemon

Instructions:

1. Steam the cauliflower and broccoli florets until tender, about 5-7 minutes. Drain and set aside.

2. In a large skillet, heat the olive oil over medium heat. Add the minced garlic and diced red onion. Sauté for 2-3 minutes until they become fragrant and slightly translucent.

3. Add the steamed cauliflower, broccoli, and chickpeas to the skillet. Sprinkle with ground cumin, ground turmeric, salt, and pepper. Cook for 5-7 minutes, stirring occasionally, until the vegetables are lightly browned and heated.

4. Squeeze the lemon juice over the mixture and stir well.

Per Serving: Calories: 250 Protein: 10g Fat: 6g Salt: 400mg

Vegan Mushroom Risotto

Total Servings: 1 serving
Preparation Time: 10 minutes
Time to Cook: 30 minutes

Ingredients:
- 1/2 cup Arborio rice
- 1 1/2 cups vegetable broth (low-sodium)
- 1/2 cup sliced mushrooms (such as cremini or shiitake)
- 1/4 cup diced onion
- 1 clove garlic, minced
- 1/4 cup dry white wine (optional)
- 1 tablespoon olive oil

- 1/2 teaspoon dried thyme
- Salt and pepper to taste
- Chopped fresh parsley for garnish (optional)

Instructions:

1. Heat the vegetable broth over low heat in a saucepan, keeping it warm but not boiling.

2. In a separate skillet, heat the olive oil over medium heat. Add the diced onion and garlic. Sauté for 2-3 minutes until they become fragrant and translucent.

3. Add the sliced mushrooms and dried thyme to the skillet. Cook for about 5 minutes until the mushrooms are tender and browned.

4. Stir in the Arborio rice and cook for 2-3 minutes, allowing it to toast slightly.

5. If using, pour in the white wine and cook for 1-2 minutes until the rice mainly absorbs it.

6. Add the warm vegetable broth to the skillet, stirring constantly, one ladle at a time. Allow each ladle of broth to be absorbed by the rice before adding more. Continue this process for about 20-25 minutes or until the rice is creamy and tender.

7. Season the risotto with salt and pepper to taste. Garnish with chopped fresh parsley if desired.

Per Serving: Calories: 350 Protein: 6g Fat: 8g Salt: 500mg

Zucchini Noodles Pesto

Total Servings: 1 serving
Preparation Time: 15 minutes
Time to Cook: 10 minutes

Ingredients:

- 1 medium zucchini, spiralized into noodles
- 1/4 cup fresh basil leaves
- 1/4 cup fresh spinach leaves
- 1/4 cup raw walnuts
- 1 clove garlic
- 2 tablespoons extra-virgin olive oil
- 1 tablespoon lemon juice
- Salt and pepper to taste

Instructions:

1. Combine the fresh basil, spinach, raw walnuts, garlic, olive oil, lemon juice, salt, and pepper in a food processor. Blend until you have a smooth pesto sauce.

2. Heat a skillet over medium-high heat and lightly sauté the zucchini noodles for 2-3 minutes until tender.

3. Transfer the zucchini noodles to a plate and top with the freshly made pesto sauce.

Per Serving: Calories: 350 Protein: 5g Fat: 30g Salt: 300mg

Vegan Lentil

Shepherd's Pie

Total Servings: 1 serving
Preparation Time: 15 minutes
Time to Cook: 40 minutes

Ingredients:

- 1/2 cup cooked green or brown lentils
- 1/2 cup mixed vegetables (carrots, peas, corn)
- 1/4 cup diced onion
- 1 clove garlic, minced
- 1/2 cup mashed sweet potatoes
- 1 tablespoon olive oil
- 1/2 teaspoon dried thyme
- Salt and pepper to taste

Instructions:

1. Preheat your oven to 350°F (175°C).

2. In a skillet, heat olive oil over medium heat. Add diced onion and minced garlic. Sauté until they become translucent.

3. Add the mixed vegetables and sauté for another 5 minutes until they soften.

4. Stir in the cooked lentils, dried thyme, salt, and pepper. Cook for an additional 2-3 minutes until everything is well combined.

5. Transfer the lentil and vegetable mixture to an oven-safe dish. Spread the mashed sweet potatoes evenly over the top.

6. Bake in the oven for 25-30 minutes or until the top is lightly browned.

Per Serving: Calories: 400 Protein: 15g Fat: 10g Salt: 500mg

Butternut Lentil Curry

Total Servings: 1 serving
Preparation Time: 15 minutes
Time to Cook: 30 minutes

Ingredients:

- 1/2 cup diced butternut squash
- 1/4 cup dried green or brown lentils
- 1/4 cup diced onion
- 1 clove garlic, minced
- 1/2 cup canned coconut milk
- 1/2 cup vegetable broth (low-sodium)
- 1 teaspoon curry powder
- 1/2 teaspoon ground turmeric
- Salt and pepper to taste
- Fresh cilantro for garnish (optional)

Instructions:

1. Combine the diced butternut squash, lentils, diced onion, minced garlic, canned coconut milk, and vegetable broth in a saucepan.

2. Add the curry powder, ground turmeric, salt, and pepper. Stir well.

3. Bring the mixture to a boil, then reduce the heat to a simmer. Cover and cook for 25-30 minutes or until the lentils and butternut squash are tender.

4. Once cooked, taste and adjust the seasoning if necessary.

5. Serve hot, garnished with fresh cilantro if desired.

Per Serving: Calories: 450 Protein: 14g Fat: 12g
Salt: 600mg

Vegan Stuffed Acorn Squash

Total Servings: 1 serving
Preparation Time: 15 minutes
Time to Cook: 45 minutes

Ingredients:

- 1 small acorn squash
- 1/2 cup cooked quinoa
- 1/2 cup cooked black beans
- 1/4 cup diced red bell pepper
- 1/4 cup diced red onion
- 1 clove garlic, minced
- 1/2 teaspoon ground cumin
- Salt and pepper to taste
- 1 tablespoon olive oil
- Fresh cilantro for garnish (optional)

Instructions:

1. Preheat your oven to 375°F (190°C).

2. Cut the acorn squash in half lengthwise and scoop out the seeds. Place the squash halves, cut side down, on a baking sheet. Bake for 30-35 minutes or until the squash is tender when pierced with a fork.

3. While the squash is roasting, heat olive oil in a skillet over medium heat. Add diced red bell pepper, red onion, and minced garlic. Sauté for 2-3 minutes until they begin to soften.

4. Add cooked quinoa, black beans, ground cumin, salt, and pepper to the skillet. Stir well and cook for another 2-3 minutes to heat everything.

5. Once the acorn squash is roasted, please remove it from the oven and flip the halves. Fill each half with the quinoa and black bean mixture.

6. Return the stuffed squash to the oven and bake for 10 minutes.

7. Garnish with fresh cilantro if desired, and serve hot.

Per Serving: Calories: 450 Protein: 14g Fat: 9g
Salt: 350mg

Vegan Black Bean Salad

Total Servings: 1 serving
Preparation Time: 15 minutes
Time to Assemble: 10 minutes

Ingredients:

- 1 cup cooked black beans
- 1/2 cup diced cucumber
- 1/2 cup diced tomato
- 1/4 cup diced red onion
- 1/4 cup chopped fresh cilantro
- 1 tablespoon extra-virgin olive oil
- 1 tablespoon fresh lime juice
- 1/2 teaspoon ground cumin
- Salt and pepper to taste
- Avocado slices for garnish (optional)

Instructions:

1. In a large bowl, combine cooked black beans, diced cucumber, tomato, red onion, and chopped fresh cilantro.

2. Whisk together olive oil, fresh lime juice, ground cumin, salt, and pepper in a separate small bowl.

3. Pour the dressing over the black bean salad and toss gently to coat.

4. Garnish with avocado slices if desired, and serve immediately.

Per Serving: Calories: 380 Protein: 15g Fat: 12g Salt: 400mg

Vegan Spinach Dip

Total Servings: 1 serving
Preparation Time: 10 minutes
Time to Cook: N/A (No cooking required)

Ingredients:

- 1/2 cup fresh spinach, finely chopped
- 1/4 cup silken tofu
- 1 clove garlic, minced
- 1 tablespoon nutritional yeast
- 1/2 teaspoon lemon juice
- Salt and pepper to taste
- Sliced veggies (such as carrots, cucumber, and bell peppers) for dipping

Instructions:

1. Combine the chopped spinach, silken tofu, minced garlic, nutritional yeast, and lemon juice in a food processor.

2. Blend until smooth, scraping down the sides of the processor as needed.

3. Season with salt and pepper to taste.

4. Transfer the spinach dip to a serving bowl.

5. Serve with an assortment of sliced veggies for dipping.

6. Enjoy your Vegan Spinach Dip!

Per Serving: Calories: Approximately 100 kcal Protein: 8g Fat: 5g Salt: To taste

Vegan Green Thai Curry

Total Servings: 1 serving
Preparation Time: 15 minutes
Time to Cook: 20 minutes

Ingredients:

- 1/2 cup cooked brown rice or quinoa
- 1/2 cup broccoli florets
- 1/4 cup diced tofu
- 1/4 cup sliced bell peppers
- 1/4 cup sliced zucchini
- 1/4 cup sliced mushrooms
- 1/4 cup canned coconut milk
- 1 tablespoon green curry paste
- 1/2 teaspoon grated ginger
- 1/2 teaspoon soy sauce or tamari
- 1/2 teaspoon agave nectar or maple syrup (optional for sweetness)
- Fresh cilantro for garnish

Instructions:

1. Add the green curry paste and grated ginger in a skillet over medium heat. Stir for a minute until fragrant.

2. Add the diced tofu and cook until lightly browned.

3. Stir in the sliced vegetables and cook for another 3-4 minutes.

4. Pour in the canned coconut milk and soy sauce (and agave nectar if using) and let it simmer for 10-15 minutes or until the vegetables are tender.

5. Serve the green Thai curry over cooked brown rice or quinoa.

6. Garnish with fresh cilantro.

7. Enjoy your Vegan Green Thai Curry!

Per Serving: Calories: Approximately 350 kcal Protein: 10g Fat: 20g Salt: To taste

Vegan Falafel Bowl

Total Servings: 1 serving
Preparation Time: 15 minutes
Time to Cook: 20 minutes

Ingredients:

- 4-5 homemade or store-bought falafel patties
- 1/2 cup cooked quinoa
- 1/4 cup diced cucumber
- 1/4 cup diced tomato
- 1/4 cup shredded lettuce
- 2 tablespoons tahini sauce
- Fresh lemon juice for drizzling
- Fresh parsley for garnish

Instructions:

1. Cook the falafel patties according to package instructions or use homemade ones.

2. In a bowl, layer cooked quinoa as the base.

3. Top with falafel patties, diced cucumber, tomato, and shredded lettuce.

4. Drizzle tahini sauce over the bowl.

5. Finish with a squeeze of fresh lemon juice and garnish with fresh parsley.

6. Enjoy your Vegan Falafel Bowl!

Per Serving: Calories: Approximately 400 kcal Protein: 12g Fat: 15g Salt: To taste

Vegan Ratatouille

Total Servings: 1 serving
Preparation Time: 15 minutes
Time to Cook: 30 minutes

Ingredients:

- 1 small eggplant, diced
- 1 small zucchini, diced
- 1 small yellow bell pepper, diced
- 1 small red bell pepper, diced
- 1 small onion, diced
- 2 cloves garlic, minced
- 1 can (14 oz) diced tomatoes
- 1 teaspoon dried basil
- 1 teaspoon dried oregano
- Salt and black pepper to taste
- Fresh basil leaves for garnish (optional)

Instructions:

1. Heat a tablespoon of olive oil in a large skillet over medium heat.

2. Add the diced eggplant, zucchini, yellow bell pepper, red bell pepper, onion, and minced garlic to the skillet.

3. Sauté the vegetables for about 10 minutes or until they begin to soften.

4. Stir in the canned diced tomatoes (with their juice), dried basil, dried oregano, salt, and black pepper.

5. Reduce the heat to low, cover the skillet, and simmer for 15-20 minutes until the vegetables are tender.

6. Adjust the seasoning if needed.

7. Serve the Vegan Ratatouille hot, garnished with fresh basil leaves if desired.

Per Serving: Calories: Approximately 250 kcal Protein: 6g Fat: 4g Salt: To taste

Chickpea Spinach Burger

Total Servings: 1 serving
Preparation Time: 15 minutes
Time to Cook: 10 minutes

Ingredients:

- 1/2 cup cooked chickpeas, mashed
- 1/2 cup spinach, finely chopped
- 2 tablespoons rolled oats
- 1/4 cup grated carrot
- 1/4 cup diced red bell pepper
- 1/2 teaspoon ground cumin
- 1/2 teaspoon paprika
- Salt and black pepper to taste
- 1 whole-grain burger bun
- Lettuce, tomato, and avocado slices for garnish (optional)

Instructions:

1. Combine the mashed chickpeas, chopped spinach, rolled oats, grated carrot, diced red bell pepper, ground cumin, paprika, salt, and black pepper in a mixing bowl.

2. Mix until all ingredients are well combined.

3. Shape the mixture into a burger patty.

4. Heat a non-stick skillet over medium heat and lightly grease it.

5. Cook the chickpea spinach burger patty for about 4-5 minutes on each side or until it›s golden brown and cooked through.

6. Toast the whole-grain burger bun in the skillet until slightly crispy.

7. Assemble your burger with lettuce, tomato, and avocado slices if desired.

8. Serve the Chickpea Spinach Burger hot.

Per Serving: Calories: Approximately 350 kcal Protein: 12g Fat: 6g Salt: To taste

Vegan Eggplant Parmesan

Total Servings: 1 serving
Preparation Time: 20 minutes
Time to Cook: 25 minutes

Ingredients:

- 1 small eggplant, thinly sliced
- 1/2 cup marinara sauce (look for low-sodium options)
- 1/4 cup breadcrumbs (preferably whole wheat)
- 2 tablespoons nutritional yeast
- 1/2 teaspoon dried basil
- 1/2 teaspoon dried oregano
- Salt and black pepper to taste
- Fresh basil leaves for garnish (optional)

Instructions:

1. Preheat your oven to 375°F (190°C).

2. Combine breadcrumbs, nutritional yeast, dried basil, dried oregano, salt, and black pepper in a bowl.

3. Dip each eggplant slice into the breadcrumb mixture, ensuring it s coated evenly.

4. Place the coated eggplant slices on a baking sheet lined with parchment paper.

5. Bake in the oven for about 15 minutes or until the eggplant is tender and the coating is crispy.

6. In a microwave-safe bowl, heat the marinara sauce for 1-2 minutes until warm.

7. Pour the warmed marinara sauce over the baked eggplant slices.

8. Garnish with fresh basil leaves if desired.

9. Serve your Vegan Eggplant Parmesan hot.

Per Serving: Calories: Approximately 250 kcal Protein: 9g Fat: 5g Salt: To taste

Vegan Tomato Basil Pasta

Total Servings: 1 serving
Preparation Time: 10 minutes
Time to Cook: 15 minutes

Ingredients:

- 1 cup whole-grain pasta
- 1 cup cherry tomatoes, halved
- 2 cloves garlic, minced
- 1/4 cup fresh basil leaves, chopped
- 1 tablespoon olive oil
- 2 tablespoons nutritional yeast (optional for added flavor)
- Salt and black pepper to taste
- Red pepper flakes for a hint of spice (optional)

Instructions:

1. Cook the whole-grain pasta according to package instructions until al dente. Drain and set aside.

2. In a skillet, heat olive oil over medium heat. Add minced garlic and sauté for about 1 minute until fragrant.

3. Add the cherry tomatoes and cook for an additional 3-4 minutes until they start to soften.

4. Toss in the cooked pasta and chopped fresh basil. Stir to combine.

5. If desired, sprinkle nutritional yeast for added flavor.

6. Season with salt and black pepper to taste. Add red pepper flakes for some heat if you like.

7. Serve your Vegan Tomato Basil Pasta hot.

Per Serving: Calories: Approximately 400 kcal Protein: 10g Fat: 10g Salt: To taste

Vegan Cauliflower Alfredo

Total Servings: 1 serving
Preparation Time: 15 minutes
Time to Cook: 20 minutes

Ingredients:

- 1 cup cauliflower florets
- 1/2 cup unsweetened almond milk
- 2 cloves garlic, minced
- 1/4 cup nutritional yeast
- 1 tablespoon olive oil
- 1/2 teaspoon dried thyme
- Salt and black pepper to taste
- 1 cup whole-grain pasta
- Fresh parsley for garnish (optional)

Instructions:

1. Steam or boil the cauliflower florets until tender. Drain and set aside.

2. Combine the steamed cauliflower, unsweetened almond milk, minced garlic, nutritional yeast, olive oil, dried thyme, salt, and black pepper in a blender.

3. Blend until you achieve a creamy consistency. If needed, add more almond milk to reach your desired thickness.

4. Cook the whole-grain pasta according to package instructions. Drain and set aside.

5. Pour the cauliflower Alfredo sauce over the cooked pasta and toss until well coated.

6. Garnish with fresh parsley if desired.

7. Serve your Vegan Cauliflower Alfredo hot.

Per Serving: Calories: Approximately 350 kcal Protein: 12g Fat: 10g Salt: To taste

Vegan Stuffed Peppers

Total Servings: 1 serving
Preparation Time: 20 minutes
Time to Cook: 40 minutes

Ingredients:

- 1 large bell pepper (any color)
- 1/2 cup cooked quinoa
- 1/2 cup canned black beans, drained and rinsed
- 1/4 cup corn kernels (frozen or canned)
- 1/4 cup diced tomatoes (canned or fresh)
- 1/4 cup diced red onion
- 1/2 teaspoon ground cumin
- 1/2 teaspoon chili powder
- Salt and pepper to taste

- 1/4 cup vegan cheese (optional)
- Fresh cilantro leaves for garnish

Instructions:

1. Preheat the Oven: Preheat your oven to 375°F (190°C).

2. Prepare the Pepper: Cut the top off the bell pepper and remove the seeds and membranes. Set aside.

3. Prepare the Filling: In a mixing bowl, combine the cooked quinoa, black beans, corn, diced tomatoes, diced red onion, ground cumin, chili powder, salt, and pepper. Mix well until all ingredients are evenly distributed.

4. Stuff the Pepper: Pack the prepared bell pepper with the quinoa and vegetable mixture tightly.

5. Bake: Cover the stuffed pepper in an oven-safe dish with aluminum foil. Bake in the oven for 30-35 minutes or until the pepper is tender.

6. Optional Cheese Topping: If desired, remove the foil, sprinkle vegan cheese over the top of the stuffed pepper, and return it to the oven for 5 minutes or until the cheese has melted and is bubbly.

7. Garnish and Serve: Remove the stuffed pepper from the oven and garnish with fresh cilantro leaves. Let it cool for a few minutes before serving.

Per Serving: Calories: 350 Protein: 11g Fat: 7g Salt: 450mg

Vegan Sweet Potato Chili

Total Servings: 1 serving
Preparation Time: 15 minutes
Time to Cook: 30 minutes

Ingredients:

- 1 medium sweet potato, peeled and diced
- 1/2 cup canned black beans, drained and rinsed
- 1/2 cup canned kidney beans, drained and rinsed
- 1/2 cup diced tomatoes (canned or fresh)
- 1/4 cup diced red onion
- 1/4 cup corn kernels (frozen or canned)
- 1/2 teaspoon chili powder
- 1/2 teaspoon ground cumin
- Salt and pepper to taste
- 1 cup vegetable broth
- Fresh cilantro leaves for garnish
- Lime wedges for garnish

Instructions:

1. Prepare the Sweet Potato: Add the diced sweet potato and vegetable broth in a medium-sized pot. Bring to a boil, then reduce the heat to a simmer. Cook for 10-15 minutes or until the sweet potato is tender.

2. Add Ingredients: Add the black beans, kidney beans, diced tomatoes, diced red onion, corn kernels, chili powder, ground cumin, salt, and pepper to the pot. Stir well to combine.

3. Simmer: Allow the chili to simmer for 10-15 minutes, stirring occasionally, until all the ingredients are heated and well blended.

4. Garnish and Serve: Serve the vegan sweet potato chili hot, garnished with fresh cilantro leaves and lime wedges.

Per Serving: Calories: 380 Protein: 12g Fat: 2g Salt: 600mg

Vegan Coconut Turmeric Rice

Total Servings: 1 serving
Preparation Time: 5 minutes
Time to Cook: 20 minutes

Ingredients:

- 1/2 cup brown rice
- 1 cup coconut milk (canned or homemade)
- 1/2 teaspoon ground turmeric
- 1/4 teaspoon ground ginger
- Salt to taste
- Fresh cilantro leaves for garnish

Instructions:

1. Rinse the Rice: Rinse the brown rice under cold water until the water runs clear. This helps remove excess starch.

2. Cook the Rice: In a medium saucepan, combine the rinsed rice, coconut milk, ground turmeric, ginger, and a pinch of salt. Stir well.

3. Simmer: Bring the mixture to a boil over medium-high heat, then reduce the heat to low, cover the saucepan, and simmer for 15-20 minutes, or until the rice is tender and has absorbed all the liquid. Stir occasionally.

4. Fluff and Garnish: Once the rice is cooked, fluff it with a fork. Garnish with fresh cilantro leaves.

Per Serving: Calories: 470 Protein: 8g Fat: 24g Salt: 300mg

Vegan Lentil Stir-Fry

Total Servings: 1 serving
Preparation Time: 15 minutes
Time to Cook: 20 minutes

Ingredients:

- 1/2 cup dried green or brown lentils
- 1 cup water
- 1/2 cup broccoli florets
- 1/2 cup bell peppers (any color), thinly sliced
- 1/2 cup carrots, julienned
- 1/4 cup snow peas, trimmed and halved
- 1/4 cup low-sodium vegetable broth
- 1 clove garlic, minced
- 1/2 teaspoon grated ginger
- 1 tablespoon low-sodium soy sauce or tamari (gluten-free option)
- 1/2 teaspoon sesame oil (optional)

- Salt and pepper to taste
- 1 tablespoon chopped green onions for garnish

Instructions:

1. Cook the Lentils: Rinse them thoroughly and place them in a saucepan with 1 cup of water. Bring to a boil, then reduce heat to low and simmer for 15-20 minutes or until lentils are tender. Drain and set aside.

2. Stir-Fry Vegetables: Heat the vegetable broth over medium-high heat in a large skillet or wok. Add the minced garlic and grated ginger, and stir for about 30 seconds until fragrant.

3. Add Vegetables: Add the broccoli, bell peppers, carrots, and snow peas to the skillet. Stir-fry for 4-5 minutes until the vegetables are tender-crisp.

4. Combine Lentils: Add the cooked lentils to the skillet and stir-fry for 2-3 minutes to heat through.

5. Season: Drizzle with soy sauce or tamari and sesame oil (if using). Season with salt and pepper to taste. Continue to stir-fry for another 2 minutes to combine flavors.

6. Serve: Transfer the vegan lentil stir-fry to a serving plate. Garnish with chopped green onions.

Per Serving: Calories: 380 Protein: 24g Fat: 2g Salt: 450mg

Vegan Cauliflower Tacos

Total Servings: 1 serving
Preparation Time: 15 minutes
Time to Cook: 25 minutes

Ingredients:

- 1 cup cauliflower florets
- 1/2 teaspoon chili powder
- 1/2 teaspoon cumin
- 1/4 teaspoon paprika
- 1/4 teaspoon garlic powder
- Salt and pepper to taste
- 2 small corn tortillas
- 1/4 cup black beans, drained and rinsed
- 1/4 cup diced tomatoes (canned or fresh)
- 1/4 cup shredded lettuce
- 1/4 cup diced avocado
- 1/4 cup diced red onion
- Fresh cilantro leaves for garnish
- Lime wedges for garnish

Instructions:

1. Roast Cauliflower: Preheat your oven to 425°F (220°C). Toss the cauliflower florets with chili powder, cumin, paprika, garlic powder, salt, and pepper. Spread them

2. on a baking sheet, roast for 20-25 minutes or until the cauliflower is tender and slightly crispy.

3. Warm Tortillas: While the cauliflower is roasting, warm the corn tortillas in a dry skillet over medium heat for about 30

seconds on each side or until pliable.

4. Assemble Tacos: Place the warm tortillas on a plate. Divide the roasted cauliflower, black beans, tomatoes, shredded lettuce, avocado, and red onion evenly between the two tortillas.

5. Garnish: Garnish the tacos with fresh cilantro leaves and serve with lime wedges for squeezing over the top.

Per Serving: Calories: 350 Protein: 8g Fat: 10g Salt: 350mg

Vegan Stuffed Potatoes

Total Servings: 1 serving
Preparation Time: 10 minutes
Time to Cook: 45 minutes

Ingredients:
- 1 medium russet potato
- 1/4 cup canned black beans, drained and rinsed
- 1/4 cup diced tomatoes (canned or fresh)
- 1/4 cup diced red onion
- 1/4 cup corn kernels (frozen or canned)
- 1/2 teaspoon ground cumin
- 1/2 teaspoon chili powder
- Salt and pepper to taste
- 1/4 cup guacamole (homemade or store-bought)
- Fresh cilantro leaves for garnish

Instructions:

1. Bake the Potato: Preheat your oven to 400°F (200°C). Scrub the potato clean and pierce it several times with a fork. Place it directly on the oven rack and bake for 40-45 minutes or until the potato is tender when pierced with a fork.

2. Prepare the Filling: While the potato is baking, in a mixing bowl, combine the black beans, diced tomatoes, diced red onion, corn kernels, ground cumin, chili powder, salt, and pepper. Mix well until all ingredients are evenly distributed.

3. Split the Potato: Remove the baked potato from the oven and let it cool for a minute. Slice it in half lengthwise, and gently fluff the insides with a fork.

4. Stuff the Potato: Spoon the prepared filling into the split potato, dividing it evenly between the two halves.

5. Garnish: Top each stuffed potato half with a dollop of guacamole and fresh cilantro leaves.

Per Serving: Calories: 400 Protein: 10g Fat: 10g Salt: 400mg

Vegan Spinach Risotto

Total Servings: 1 serving
Preparation Time: 10 minutes
Time to Cook: 30 minutes

Ingredients:
- 1/2 cup Arborio rice

- 2 cups vegetable broth (low-sodium)
- 1/4 cup diced onion
- 1 clove garlic, minced
- 1/4 cup dry white wine (optional)
- 1/2 cup fresh spinach leaves, chopped
- 1/4 cup nutritional yeast (optional for a cheesy flavor)
- Salt and pepper to taste
- 1 tablespoon olive oil
- Fresh basil leaves for garnish (optional)

Instructions:

1. Prepare the Broth: Warm the vegetable broth over low heat in a saucepan. Keep it simmering while you prepare the risotto.

2. Sauté Onion and Garlic: Heat the olive oil over medium heat in a separate large skillet. Add the diced onion and sauté for 2-3 minutes until it becomes translucent. Add the minced garlic and cook for an additional 30 seconds until fragrant.

3. Toast the Rice: Add the Arborio rice to the skillet with the onion and garlic. Stir constantly for 1-2 minutes until the rice is lightly toasted.

4. Deglaze with Wine (Optional): If using white wine, pour it into the skillet and stir until the rice mainly absorbs it.

5. Cook the Risotto: Add the warm vegetable broth, one ladle at a time, to the skillet with the rice. Stir constantly and allow the liquid to be absorbed before adding more broth. Continue this process for 20-25 minutes until the rice is creamy and tender.

6. Add Spinach and Nutritional Yeast: Stir in the chopped spinach and nutritional yeast (if using) during the last few minutes of cooking. Cook until the spinach is wilted and the risotto is creamy.

7. Season and Serve: Season the risotto with salt and pepper to taste. Transfer it to a serving plate and garnish with fresh basil leaves if desired.

Per Serving: Calories: 350 Protein: 7g Fat: 7g Salt: 800mg

Vegan Quinoa Enchiladas

Total Servings: 1 serving
Preparation Time: 20 minutes
Time to Cook: 25 minutes

Ingredients:
For the Filling:
- 1/2 cup cooked quinoa
- 1/4 cup black beans, drained and rinsed
- 1/4 cup corn kernels (frozen or canned)
- 1/4 cup diced bell peppers (any color)
- 1/4 cup diced red onion

- 1/2 teaspoon ground cumin
- 1/2 teaspoon chili powder
- Salt and pepper to taste

For the Enchilada Sauce:
- 1/2 cup tomato sauce
- 1/2 teaspoon ground cumin
- 1/2 teaspoon chili powder
- Salt and pepper to taste

For Assembly:
- 2 small corn tortillas
- 1/4 cup vegan shredded cheese (optional)
- Chopped fresh cilantro leaves for garnish

Instructions:

1. Prepare the Quinoa: In a mixing bowl, combine the cooked quinoa, black beans, corn kernels, diced bell peppers, diced red onion, ground cumin, chili powder, salt, and pepper. Mix well until all ingredients are evenly distributed.

2. Make the Enchilada Sauce: In a separate bowl, mix the tomato sauce, ground cumin, chili powder, salt, and pepper to create the enchilada sauce.

3. Preheat the Oven: Preheat your oven to 350°F (175°C).

4. Assemble the Enchiladas: Warm the corn tortillas in a dry skillet over medium heat for 30 seconds on each side or until pliable. Lay them flat and divide the quinoa filling between the tortillas. Roll them up tightly and place them seam-side down in an ovenproof dish.

5. Pour the Sauce: Pour the enchilada sauce over the rolled tortillas, ensuring they are well-covered. Sprinkle vegan shredded cheese on top if desired.

6. Bake: Place the dish in the preheated oven and bake for 15-20 minutes or until the enchiladas are heated and the cheese (if used) is melted and bubbly.

7. Garnish and Serve: Remove from the oven, garnish with chopped fresh cilantro leaves, and serve hot.

Per Serving: Calories: 380 Protein: 10g Fat: 6g Salt: 700mg

Chapter 7: Soups

Turmeric Veggie Lentil Soup

Total Servings: 1 serving
Preparation Time: 15 minutes
Time to Cook: 30 minutes

Ingredients:

- 1/2 cup dried green or brown lentils
- 2 cups low-sodium vegetable broth
- 1/2 cup diced carrots
- 1/2 cup diced celery
- 1/2 cup diced onion
- 1/2 cup diced bell peppers (any color)
- 1 clove garlic, minced
- 1/2 teaspoon ground turmeric
- 1/2 teaspoon ground cumin
- Salt and pepper to taste
- Fresh parsley leaves for garnish (optional)

Instructions:

1. Rinse the Lentils: Rinse the lentils thoroughly under cold water and drain.

2. Prepare the Broth: Combine the vegetable broth and rinsed lentils in a large pot. Bring to a boil, then reduce heat to low, cover, and simmer for 15-20 minutes or until the lentils are tender.

3. Sauté the Vegetables: Heat a little water or olive oil over medium heat in a separate skillet. Add the diced carrots, celery, onion, and bell peppers. Sauté for 5-7 minutes until the vegetables begin to soften.

4. Add Garlic and Spices: Add the minced garlic, turmeric, ground cumin, salt, and pepper to the sautéed vegetables. Cook for an additional 1-2 minutes until fragrant.

5. Combine Ingredients: Transfer the sautéed vegetables to the pot with the cooked lentils. Stir well to combine all ingredients. Continue simmering for an additional 5 minutes to meld the flavors.

6. Serve: Ladle the turmeric veggie lentil soup into a bowl. Garnish with fresh parsley leaves if desired.

Per Serving: Calories: 350 Protein: 18g Fat: 1g Salt: 800mg

Creamy Turmeric Cauliflower Soup

Total Servings: 1 serving
Preparation Time: 10 minutes
Time to Cook: 30 minutes

Ingredients:

- 1 cup cauliflower florets
- 1/2 cup diced onions
- 1/2 cup diced carrots
- 1 clove garlic, minced
- 2 cups low-sodium vegetable broth
- 1/2 teaspoon ground turmeric
- 1/2 teaspoon ground ginger
- Salt and pepper to taste
- 1/4 cup canned coconut milk (total fat)
- Fresh cilantro leaves for garnish (optional)

Instructions:

1. Sauté the Vegetables: In a large pot, sauté the diced onions, carrots, and minced garlic over medium heat until they soften, about 5-7 minutes.

2. Add Cauliflower: Add the cauliflower florets to the pot and continue to sauté for 2-3 minutes.

3. Season: Stir in the ground turmeric, ground ginger, salt, and pepper.

4. Add Broth: Pour in the vegetable broth, making sure the vegetables are submerged. Bring to a boil, then reduce heat to low, cover, and simmer for 15-20 minutes or until the vegetables are tender.

5. Blend Soup: Using an immersion or regular blender (blend in batches if necessary), puree the soup until smooth and creamy.

6. Add Coconut Milk: Return the soup to the pot and stir in the canned coconut milk. Heat gently over low heat, stirring until well combined and heated through.

7. Serve: Ladle the creamy turmeric cauliflower soup into a bowl. Garnish with fresh cilantro leaves if desired.

Per Serving: Calories: 280 Protein: 4g Fat: 12g Salt: 800mg

Tomato Basil Quinoa Soup

Total Servings: 1 serving
Preparation Time: 15 minutes
Time to Cook: 25 minutes

Ingredients:

- 1/4 cup quinoa, rinsed and drained
- 1 cup low-sodium vegetable broth
- 1/2 cup diced tomatoes (canned or fresh)
- 1/4 cup diced onion
- 1/4 cup diced carrots
- 1/4 cup diced celery
- 1 clove garlic, minced
- 1/2 teaspoon dried basil
- Salt and pepper to taste
- Fresh basil leaves for garnish (optional)

Instructions:

1. Cook Quinoa: Combine the quinoa and vegetable broth in a small saucepan. Bring to a boil, then reduce heat to low, cover, and simmer for 15-20 minutes or until the quinoa is tender and the liquid is absorbed.

2. Sauté Vegetables: Heat a little water or olive oil over medium heat in a separate skillet. Add the diced onion, carrots, celery, and minced garlic. Sauté for 5-7 minutes until the vegetables start to soften.

3. Combine Ingredients: Add the sautéed vegetables, diced tomatoes, dried basil, salt, and pepper to the pot with the cooked quinoa. Stir well to combine all ingredients.

4. Simmer: Simmer the tomato basil quinoa soup for 5-7 minutes to blend flavors.

5. Serve: Ladle the soup into a bowl. Garnish with fresh basil leaves if desired.

Per Serving: Calories: 280 Protein: 6g Fat: 2g Salt: 750mg

Spicy Sweet Potato Soup

Total Servings: 1 serving
Preparation Time: 15 minutes
Time to Cook: 30 minutes

Ingredients:

- 1 medium sweet potato, peeled and diced
- 1/4 cup diced onion
- 1/4 cup diced red bell pepper
- 1 clove garlic, minced
- 1/2 teaspoon ground cumin
- 1/4 teaspoon chili powder
- 1/4 teaspoon cayenne pepper (adjust to taste)
- Salt and pepper to taste

- 2 cups low-sodium vegetable broth
- 1/4 cup canned coconut milk (total fat)
- Fresh cilantro leaves for garnish (optional)

Instructions:

1. Prepare Sweet Potato: In a large pot, combine the diced sweet potato, onion, red bell pepper, and minced garlic.

2. Sauté: Sauté the vegetables over medium heat for 5-7 minutes until they soften.

3. Season: Add the ground cumin, chili powder, cayenne, salt, and pepper to the pot. Stir well to coat the vegetables with the spices.

4. Add Broth: Pour in the low-sodium vegetable broth and bring the mixture to a boil. Reduce heat to low, cover, and simmer for 15-20 minutes or until the sweet potatoes are tender.

5. Blend: Use an immersion blender or transfer the soup to a regular blender (blend in batches if necessary) and puree until smooth and creamy.

6. Add Coconut Milk: Return the soup to the pot and stir in the canned coconut milk. Heat gently over low heat, stirring until well combined and heated through.

7. Serve: Ladle the spicy sweet potato soup into a bowl. Garnish with fresh cilantro leaves if desired.

Per Serving: Calories: 280 Protein: 4g Fat: 10g Salt: 800mg

Mushroom Thyme Rice Soup

Total Servings: 1 serving
Preparation Time: 15 minutes
Time to Cook: 30 minutes

Ingredients:

- 1/2 cup sliced mushrooms (any variety)
- 1/4 cup diced onion
- 1/4 cup diced celery
- 1/4 cup diced carrots
- 1 clove garlic, minced
- 1/2 teaspoon dried thyme
- Salt and pepper to taste
- 1/4 cup brown rice
- 2 cups low-sodium vegetable broth
- 1/4 cup unsweetened almond milk
- Fresh parsley leaves for garnish (optional)

Instructions:

1. Sauté Vegetables: In a large pot, sauté the sliced mushrooms, diced onion, celery, and carrots over medium heat until they soften, about 5-7 minutes.

2. Add Garlic and Thyme: Add the minced garlic, dried thyme, salt, and pepper to the pot. Stir for an additional minute until fragrant.

3. Add Rice and Broth: Stir in the brown rice and low-sodium

vegetable broth. Bring the mixture to a boil, then reduce heat to low, cover, and simmer for 20-25 minutes or until the rice is tender.

4. Blend: Use an immersion blender or transfer half of the soup to a regular blender (blend in batches if necessary) and puree until smooth. Return the pureed portion to the pot.

5. Add Almond Milk: Stir in the unsweetened almond milk and heat gently over low heat until well combined and heated through.

6. Serve: Ladle the mushroom thyme rice soup into a bowl. Garnish with fresh parsley leaves if desired.

Per Serving: Calories: 300 Protein: 7g Fat: 4g Salt: 700mg

Lemongrass Carrot Soup

Total Servings: 1 serving
Preparation Time: 10 minutes
Time to Cook: 25 minutes

Ingredients:

- 1/2 cup diced carrots
- 1/4 cup diced onion
- 1 clove garlic, minced
- 1/2 teaspoon grated fresh ginger
- 1 stalk lemongrass, cut into 2-inch pieces
- Salt and pepper to taste
- 2 cups low-sodium vegetable broth
- 1/4 cup canned coconut milk (total fat)
- Fresh cilantro leaves for garnish (optional)

Instructions:

1. Sauté Vegetables: In a large pot, sauté the diced carrots and diced onion over medium heat until they soften, about 5-7 minutes.

2. Add Garlic and Ginger to the pot with the minced garlic and grated fresh ginger. Stir for an additional minute until fragrant.

3. Lemongrass Infusion: Add the lemongrass pieces to the pot. This will infuse the soup with a subtle lemongrass flavor.

4. Season: Season with salt and pepper to taste.

5. Add Broth: Pour in the low-sodium vegetable broth. Bring the mixture to a boil, then reduce heat to low, cover, and simmer for 15-20 minutes or until the carrots are tender.

6. Remove Lemongrass: Remove the lemongrass pieces from the pot and discard.

7. Blend: Use an immersion blender or transfer the soup to a regular blender (blend in batches if necessary) and puree until smooth.

8. Add Coconut Milk: Stir in the canned coconut milk and heat gently over low heat until well combined and heated through.

9. Serve: Ladle the lemongrass carrot soup into a bowl.

Garnish with fresh cilantro leaves if desired.

Per Serving: Calories: 250 Protein: 3g Fat: 8g Salt: 800mg

Creamy Spinach Avocado Soup

Total Servings: 1 serving
Preparation Time: 10 minutes
Time to Cook: 15 minutes

Ingredients:

- 1/2 ripe avocado
- 1 cup fresh spinach leaves
- 1/4 cup diced onion
- 1 clove garlic, minced
- 1 cup low-sodium vegetable broth
- 1/4 cup unsweetened almond milk
- Juice of 1/2 lemon
- Salt and pepper to taste
- Fresh basil leaves for garnish (optional)

Instructions:

1. Blend Ingredients: In a blender, combine the ripe avocado, fresh spinach leaves, diced onion, minced garlic, low-sodium vegetable broth, unsweetened almond milk, and lemon juice.

2. Blend until Smooth: Blend until the mixture is smooth and creamy, scraping down the sides of the blender as needed.

3. Heat Soup: Pour the blended soup into a saucepan and gently heat it over low heat. Stir occasionally to prevent sticking.

4. Season: Season the soup with salt and pepper to taste. Adjust the seasoning as needed.

5. Serve: Ladle the creamy spinach avocado soup into a bowl. Garnish with fresh basil leaves if desired.

Per Serving: Calories: 250 Protein: 5g Fat: 20g Salt: 700mg

Roasted Pepper Chickpea Soup

Total Servings: 1 serving
Preparation Time: 15 minutes
Time to Cook: 25 minutes

Ingredients:

- 1/2 cup roasted red bell peppers (from a jar or homemade)
- 1/2 cup cooked chickpeas
- 1/4 cup diced onion
- 1 clove garlic, minced
- 1 cup low-sodium vegetable broth
- 1/4 cup unsweetened coconut milk
- 1/2 teaspoon smoked paprika
- Salt and pepper to taste

- Fresh cilantro leaves for garnish (optional)

Instructions:

1. Sauté Vegetables: In a saucepan, sauté the diced onion and minced garlic over medium heat until they become translucent, about 5 minutes.

2. Add Peppers and Chickpeas: Add the roasted red bell peppers and cooked chickpeas to the saucepan. Sauté for an additional 2-3 minutes.

3. Blend Ingredients: Transfer the sautéed mixture to a blender. Add the low-sodium vegetable broth, unsweetened coconut milk, and smoked paprika. Blend until smooth.

4. Heat Soup: Pour the blended soup back into the saucepan and gently heat it over low heat. Stir occasionally.

5. Season: Season the soup with salt and pepper to taste. Adjust the seasoning as needed.

6. Serve: Ladle the roasted pepper chickpea soup into a bowl. Garnish with fresh cilantro leaves if desired.

Per Serving: Calories: 320 Protein: 8g Fat: 14g Salt: 800mg

Butternut Apple Soup

Total Servings: 1 serving
Preparation Time: 15 minutes
Time to Cook: 30 minutes

Ingredients:

- 1 cup diced butternut squash
- 1/2 cup diced apple (any variety)
- 1/4 cup diced onion
- 1 clove garlic, minced
- 1 cup low-sodium vegetable broth
- 1/4 cup unsweetened almond milk
- 1/2 teaspoon ground cinnamon
- Salt and pepper to taste
- Chopped fresh sage leaves for garnish (optional)

Instructions:

1. Sauté Vegetables: In a saucepan, sauté the diced butternut squash, apple, and diced onion over medium heat until they soften, about 5-7 minutes.

2. Add Garlic: Add the minced garlic and sauté for an additional minute until fragrant.

3. Blend Ingredients: Transfer the sautéed mixture to a blender. Add the low-sodium vegetable broth, unsweetened almond milk, and ground cinnamon. Blend until smooth.

4. Heat Soup: Pour the blended soup back into the saucepan and gently heat it over low heat. Stir occasionally.

5. Season: Season the soup with salt and pepper to taste. Adjust the seasoning as needed.

6. Serve: Ladle the butternut apple soup into a bowl. Garnish with chopped fresh sage leaves if desired.

Per Serving: Calories: 280 Protein: 4g Fat: 8g Salt: 700mg

Lemon Herb Lentil Soup

Total Servings: 1 serving
Preparation Time: 10 minutes
Time to Cook: 25 minutes

Ingredients:

- 1/2 cup dried green or brown lentils
- 2 cups low-sodium vegetable broth
- 1/4 cup diced carrots
- 1/4 cup diced celery
- 1/4 cup diced onion
- 1 clove garlic, minced
- 1/2 lemon, juiced
- 1/2 teaspoon dried thyme
- Salt and pepper to taste
- Fresh parsley leaves for garnish (optional)

Instructions:

1. Rinse the Lentils: Rinse the lentils thoroughly under cold water and drain.

2. Prepare the Broth: Combine the vegetable broth and rinsed lentils in a large pot. Bring to a boil, then reduce heat to low, cover, and simmer for 15-20 minutes or until the lentils are tender.

3. Sauté the Vegetables: Heat a little water or olive oil over medium heat in a separate skillet. Add the diced carrots, celery, and onion. Sauté for 5-7 minutes until the vegetables begin to soften.

4. Add Garlic and Thyme: Add the minced garlic, dried thyme, salt, and pepper to the sautéed vegetables. Cook for an additional 1-2 minutes until fragrant.

5. Combine Ingredients: Transfer the sautéed vegetables to the pot with the cooked lentils. Stir well to combine all ingredients.

6. Add Lemon Juice: Squeeze the juice of half a lemon into the soup and stir.

7. Serve: Ladle the lemon herb lentil soup into a bowl. Garnish with fresh parsley leaves if desired.

Per Serving: Calories: 280 Protein: 16g Fat: 2g Salt: 600mg

Mexican Black Bean Soup

Total Servings: 1 serving
Preparation Time: 15 minutes
Time to Cook: 25 minutes

Ingredients:

- 1/2 cup canned black beans, drained and rinsed
- 1/4 cup diced onion
- 1/4 cup diced bell peppers (any color)
- 1/4 cup diced tomatoes (canned or fresh)
- 1 clove garlic, minced

- 1/2 teaspoon ground cumin
- 1/4 teaspoon chili powder
- Salt and pepper to taste
- 1 cup low-sodium vegetable broth
- 1/4 avocado, diced, for garnish (optional)
- Fresh cilantro leaves for garnish (optional)

Instructions:

1. Sauté Vegetables: In a saucepan, sauté the diced onion, bell peppers, and minced garlic over medium heat until they become translucent, about 5 minutes.

2. Add Spices and Tomatoes: Add the ground cumin, chili powder, diced tomatoes, salt, and pepper to the sautéed vegetables. Stir well.

3. Add Black Beans and Broth: Add the drained and rinsed black beans and low-sodium vegetable broth to the saucepan. Stir to combine.

4. Simmer: Simmer the Mexican black bean soup for 15-20 minutes to allow the flavors to meld and the soup to thicken slightly.

5. Season: Adjust the seasoning with salt and pepper to taste.

6. Serve: Ladle the soup into a bowl. Garnish with diced avocado and fresh cilantro leaves if desired.

Per Serving: Calories: 320 Protein: 10g Fat: 8g Salt: 700mg

Cilantro Lime Gazpacho

Total Servings: 1 serving
Preparation Time: 10 minutes
Time to Serve: Chilled (30 minutes or longer)

Ingredients:

- 1 cup diced tomatoes
- 1/4 cup diced cucumber
- 1/4 cup diced red bell pepper
- 1/4 cup diced onion
- 1 clove garlic, minced
- 1/4 cup fresh cilantro leaves
- Juice of 1 lime
- 1/4 teaspoon ground cumin
- Salt and pepper to taste
- 1/4 avocado, diced, for garnish (optional)

Instructions:

1. Prepare Ingredients: In a blender or food processor, combine the diced tomatoes, cucumber, red bell pepper, onion, minced garlic, fresh cilantro leaves, lime juice, ground cumin, salt, and pepper.

2. Blend: Pulse the mixture until you achieve your desired consistency. Some prefer a chunkier soup, while others prefer it smoother.

3. Chill: Transfer the gazpacho to a container and refrigerate for at least 30 minutes before serving. Chilling allows the flavors to meld.

4. Serve: Ladle the chilled cilantro lime gazpacho into a bowl. Garnish with diced avocado if desired.

Per Serving: Calories: 150 Protein: 3g Fat: 7g Salt: 600mg

Roasted Garlic Potato Soup

Total Servings: 1 serving
Preparation Time: 15 minutes
Time to Cook: 35 minutes

Ingredients:

- 1 cup diced potatoes (peeled or unpeeled)
- 1/4 cup diced onion
- 1 clove garlic, roasted and minced
- 1 cup low-sodium vegetable broth
- 1/4 cup unsweetened almond milk
- 1/2 teaspoon dried thyme
- Salt and pepper to taste
- Fresh chives for garnish (optional)

Instructions:

1. Roast Garlic: Preheat your oven to 375°F (190°C). Cut the top off a garlic bulb, drizzle with olive oil, wrap it in aluminum foil, and roast for 30-35 minutes until the cloves are soft and caramelized. Once cooled, squeeze out the roasted garlic and mince it.

2. Sauté Vegetables: In a saucepan, sauté the diced potatoes and diced onion over medium heat until the onion becomes translucent, about 5 minutes.

3. Add Roasted Garlic: Stir in the minced roasted garlic and sauté for an additional minute.

4. Add Broth: Pour the low-sodium vegetable broth and the dried thyme. Bring to a boil, then reduce heat to low, cover, and simmer for 20-25 minutes until the potatoes are tender.

5. Blend Soup: Use an immersion blender or transfer the soup to a regular blender (blend in batches if necessary) and puree until smooth and creamy.

6. Add Almond Milk: Return the soup to the saucepan and stir in the unsweetened almond milk. Heat gently over low heat until well combined and heated through.

7. Season: Season the soup with salt and pepper to taste. Adjust the seasoning as needed.

8. Serve: Ladle the roasted garlic potato soup into a bowl. Garnish with fresh chives if desired.

Per Serving: Calories: 28 Protein: 6g Fat: 4g Salt: 700mg

Creamy Almond Broccoli Soup

Total Servings: 1 serving
Preparation Time: 10 minutes
Time to Cook: 20 minutes

Ingredients:

- 1 cup broccoli florets
- 1/4 cup diced onion
- 1 clove garlic, minced
- 1 cup low-sodium vegetable broth
- 1/4 cup unsweetened almond milk
- 1/2 teaspoon dried basil
- Salt and pepper to taste
- Slivered almonds for garnish (optional)

Instructions:

1. Sauté Vegetables: In a saucepan, sauté the broccoli florets, diced onion, and minced garlic over medium heat until the onion becomes translucent, about 5 minutes.

2. Add Broth: Pour the low-sodium vegetable broth and the dried basil. Bring to a boil, then reduce heat to low, cover, and simmer for 15-20 minutes until the broccoli is tender.

3. Blend Soup: Use an immersion blender or transfer the soup to a regular blender (blend in batches if necessary) and puree until smooth and creamy.

4. Add Almond Milk: Return the soup to the saucepan and stir in the unsweetened almond milk. Heat gently over low heat until well combined and heated through.

5. Season: Season the soup with salt and pepper to taste. Adjust the seasoning as needed.

6. Serve: Ladle the creamy almond broccoli soup into a bowl. Garnish with slivered almonds if desired.

Per Serving: Calories: 220 Protein: 6g Fat: 8g Salt: 700mg

Spiced Chickpea Spinach Soup

Total Servings: 1 serving
Preparation Time: 10 minutes
Time to Cook: 20 minutes

Ingredients:

- 1/2 cup canned chickpeas, drained and rinsed
- 1 cup fresh spinach leaves
- 1/4 cup diced onion
- 1 clove garlic, minced
- 1/2 teaspoon ground cumin
- 1/4 teaspoon ground coriander
- 1/4 teaspoon smoked paprika
- Salt and pepper to taste
- 1 cup low-sodium vegetable broth
- 1/4 lemon, juiced
- Fresh cilantro leaves for garnish (optional)

Instructions:

1. Sauté Vegetables: In a saucepan, sauté the diced onion and minced garlic over medium heat until they become translucent, about 5 minutes.

2. Add Spices: Stir in the ground cumin, coriander, smoked paprika, salt, and pepper. Cook for an additional minute until fragrant.

3. Add Chickpeas and Spinach: Add the canned chickpeas, fresh spinach leaves, and low-sodium vegetable broth to the saucepan. Stir well.

4. Simmer: Simmer the spiced chickpea spinach soup for 15-20 minutes until the chickpeas are tender and the spinach is wilted.

5. Add Lemon Juice: Squeeze the juice of a quarter lemon into the soup and stir.

6. Serve: Ladle the soup into a bowl. Garnish with fresh cilantro leaves if desired.

Per Serving: Calories: 260 Protein: 8g Fat: 4g Salt: 700mg

Coconut Lemongrass Soup

Total Servings: 1 serving
Preparation Time: 10 minutes
Time to Cook: 20 minutes

Ingredients:

- 1/2 cup diced tofu
- 1/4 cup sliced mushrooms (shiitake or any variety)
- 1/4 cup sliced red bell pepper
- 1/4 cup sliced snow peas
- 1 clove garlic, minced
- 1 stalk lemongrass, cut into 2-inch pieces
- 1/4 teaspoon grated fresh ginger
- 1 cup low-sodium vegetable broth
- 1/4 cup canned coconut milk (total fat)
- Salt and pepper to taste
- Fresh cilantro leaves for garnish (optional)

Instructions:

1. Sauté Tofu and Vegetables: In a saucepan, sauté the diced tofu, sliced mushrooms, sliced red bell pepper, sliced snow peas, minced garlic, and grated fresh ginger over medium heat for 5-7 minutes until vegetables are tender.

2. Lemongrass Infusion: Add the lemongrass pieces to the pot. This will infuse the soup with a subtle lemongrass flavor.

3. Add Broth: Pour in the low-sodium vegetable broth and bring the mixture to a boil. Then, reduce heat to low, cover, and simmer for 15 minutes.

4. Remove Lemongrass: Remove the lemongrass pieces

from the pot and discard.

5. Add Coconut Milk: Stir in the canned coconut milk and heat gently over low heat until well combined and heated through.

6. Season: Season the soup with salt and pepper to taste. Adjust the seasoning as needed.

7. Serve: Ladle the coconut lemongrass soup into a bowl. Garnish with fresh cilantro leaves if desired.

Per Serving: Calories: 300 Protein: 10g Fat: 16g Salt: 800mg

Miso Shiitake Mushroom Soup

Total Servings: 1 serving
Preparation Time: 10 minutes
Time to Cook: 20 minutes

Ingredients:
- 1/2 cup sliced shiitake mushrooms
- 1/4 cup diced tofu
- 1/4 cup sliced green onions
- 1 clove garlic, minced
- 1 tablespoon white miso paste
- 1 cup low-sodium vegetable broth
- 1/4 teaspoon grated fresh ginger
- 1/4 teaspoon soy sauce or tamari (optional for added flavor)
- Salt and pepper to taste
- Toasted sesame seeds for garnish (optional)

Instructions:

1. Sauté Mushrooms: In a saucepan, sauté the sliced shiitake mushrooms and minced garlic over medium heat for 5-7 minutes until they soften.

2. Add Tofu and Green Onions: Stir in the diced and sliced green onions. Sauté for an additional 2-3 minutes.

3. Dissolve Miso Paste: Dissolve the white miso paste in a small amount of hot water, then add it to the saucepan.

4. Add Broth: Pour in the low-sodium vegetable broth and add the grated fresh ginger and soy sauce or tamari (if using).

5. Simmer: Simmer the miso shiitake mushroom soup for 15 minutes to allow the flavors to meld.

6. Season: Season the soup with salt and pepper to taste. Adjust the seasoning as needed.

7. Serve: Ladle the soup into a bowl. Garnish with toasted sesame seeds if desired.

Per Serving: Calories: 220 Protein: 12g Fat: 6g Salt: 700mg

Turmeric Pumpkin Soup

Total Servings: 1 serving
Preparation Time: 10 minutes
Time to Cook: 25 minutes

Ingredients:
- 1 cup diced pumpkin
- 1/4 cup diced onion
- 1 clove garlic, minced
- 1/2 teaspoon ground turmeric
- 1/4 teaspoon ground ginger
- 1 cup low-sodium vegetable broth
- 1/4 cup unsweetened coconut milk
- Salt and pepper to taste
- Fresh cilantro leaves for garnish (optional)

Instructions:

1. Sauté Vegetables: In a saucepan, sauté the diced pumpkin and diced onion over medium heat until the onion becomes translucent, about 5 minutes.

2. Add Spices: Stir in the minced garlic, ground turmeric, and ground ginger. Cook for an additional minute until fragrant.

3. Add Broth: Pour in the low-sodium vegetable broth and bring the mixture to a boil. Then, reduce heat to low, cover, and simmer for 15-20 minutes until the pumpkin is tender.

4. Blend Soup: Use an immersion blender or transfer the soup to a regular blender (blend in batches if necessary) and puree until smooth and creamy.

5. Add Coconut Milk: Return the soup to the saucepan and stir in the unsweetened coconut milk. Heat gently over low heat until well combined and heated through.

6. Season: Season the soup with salt and pepper to taste. Adjust the seasoning as needed.

7. Serve: Ladle the turmeric pumpkin soup into a bowl. Garnish with fresh cilantro leaves if desired.

Per Serving: Calories: 280 Protein: 6g Fat: 8g Salt: 700mg

Creamy Asparagus Artichoke Soup

Total Servings: 1 serving
Preparation Time: 10 minutes
Time to Cook: 25 minutes

Ingredients:
- 1/2 cup fresh asparagus spears, trimmed and chopped
- 1/4 cup diced onion
- 1/4 cup chopped canned artichoke hearts (packed in water)
- 1 clove garlic, minced
- 1/4 cup unsalted raw cashews
- 1 cup low-sodium vegetable broth
- 1/4 cup unsweetened almond milk
- Salt and pepper to taste
- Fresh parsley leaves for garnish (optional)

Instructions:

1. Sauté Vegetables: In a saucepan, sauté the chopped asparagus, diced onion, and minced garlic over medium heat until the onion becomes translucent, about 5 minutes.

2. Add Artichokes: Stir in the chopped hearts and cook for 2-3 minutes.

3. Blend Cashews: Combine the unsalted raw cashews and low-sodium vegetable broth in a blender. Blend until the cashews are fully incorporated, and the mixture is smooth.

4. Blend Soup: Add the sautéed vegetables to the blender with the cashew and broth mixture. Blend until smooth.

5. Add Almond Milk: Return the blended soup to the saucepan and stir in the unsweetened almond milk. Heat gently over low heat until well combined and heated through.

6. Season: Season the soup with salt and pepper to taste. Adjust the seasoning as needed.

7. Serve: Ladle the creamy asparagus artichoke soup into a bowl. Garnish with fresh parsley leaves if desired.

Per Serving: Calories: 320 Protein: 8g Fat: 14g Salt: 600mg

Ginger Carrot Soup

Total Servings: 1 serving
Preparation Time: 10 minutes
Time to Cook: 25 minutes

Ingredients:
- 1 cup diced carrots
- 1/4 cup diced onion
- 1 clove garlic, minced
- 1/4 teaspoon grated fresh ginger
- 1 cup low-sodium vegetable broth
- 1/4 cup unsweetened almond milk
- Salt and pepper to taste
- Fresh chives for garnish (optional)

Instructions:

1. Sauté Vegetables: In a saucepan, sauté the diced carrots and diced onion over medium heat until the onion becomes translucent, about 5 minutes.

2. Add Ginger and Garlic: Stir in the minced garlic and grated fresh ginger. Cook for an additional minute until fragrant.

3. Add Broth: Pour in the low-sodium vegetable broth and bring the mixture to a boil. Then, reduce heat to low, cover, and simmer for 15-20 minutes until the carrots are tender.

4. Blend Soup: Use an immersion blender or transfer the soup to a regular blender (blend in batches if necessary) and puree until smooth and creamy.

5. Add Almond Milk: Return the soup to the saucepan and stir in the unsweetened almond milk. Heat gently over low heat until well combined and heated through.

6. Season: Season the soup with salt and pepper to taste. Adjust the seasoning as needed.

7. Serve: Ladle the ginger carrot soup into a bowl. Garnish with fresh chives if desired.

Per Serving: Calories: 250 Protein: 6 Fat: 4g Salt: 700mg

Lentil Spinach Minestrone

Total Servings: 1 serving
Preparation Time: 10 minutes
Time to Cook: 30 minutes

Ingredients:
- 1/4 cup brown or green lentils, rinsed
- 1/4 cup diced onion
- 1/4 cup diced carrots
- 1/4 cup diced celery
- 1 clove garlic, minced
- 1/2 cup canned diced tomatoes
- 1/2 teaspoon dried basil
- 1/4 teaspoon dried oregano
- Salt and pepper to taste
- 2 cups low-sodium vegetable broth
- 1 cup fresh spinach leaves
- Fresh parsley leaves for garnish (optional)

Instructions:

1. Sauté Vegetables: In a saucepan, sauté the diced onion, carrots, and celery over medium heat until they soften slightly, about 5 minutes.

2. Add Garlic and Herbs: Stir in the minced garlic, dried basil, oregano, salt, and pepper. Cook for an additional minute until fragrant.

3. Add Lentils and Tomatoes: Add the rinsed lentils and canned diced tomatoes to the saucepan. Stir well.

4. Pour in Broth: Pour in the low-sodium vegetable broth and bring the mixture to a boil. Then, reduce heat to low, cover, and simmer for 20-25 minutes until the lentils are tender.

5. Add Spinach: Add the fresh spinach leaves to the soup and cook for 2-3 minutes until wilted.

6. Season: Taste the soup and adjust the seasoning with salt and pepper.

7. Serve: Ladle the lentil spinach minestrone into a bowl. Garnish with fresh parsley leaves if desired.

Per Serving: Calories: 270 Protein: 14g Fat: 1g Salt: 600mg

Moroccan Chickpea Soup

Total Servings: 1 serving
Preparation Time: 10 minutes
Time to Cook: 25 minutes

Ingredients:
- 1/2 cup canned chickpeas, drained and rinsed

- 1/4 cup diced onion
- 1/4 cup diced carrots
- 1/4 cup diced bell peppers (any color)
- 1 clove garlic, minced
- 1/2 teaspoon ground cumin
- 1/4 teaspoon ground coriander
- 1/4 teaspoon ground cinnamon
- Salt and pepper to taste
- 2 cups low-sodium vegetable broth
- 1/4 cup canned diced tomatoes
- 1/4 lemon, juiced
- Fresh cilantro leaves for garnish (optional)

Instructions:

1. Sauté Vegetables: In a saucepan, sauté the diced onion, carrots, and bell peppers over medium heat until they become slightly softened, about 5 minutes.

2. Add Garlic and Spices: Stir in the minced garlic, ground cumin, ground coriander, ground cinnamon, salt, and pepper. Cook for an additional minute until fragrant.

3. Add Chickpeas and Broth: Add the canned chickpeas, low-sodium vegetable broth, and canned diced tomatoes to the saucepan. Stir well.

4. Simmer: Simmer the Moroccan chickpea soup for 15-20 minutes to allow the flavors to meld.

5. Add Lemon Juice: Squeeze the juice of a quarter lemon into the soup and stir.

6. Serve: Ladle the soup into a bowl. Garnish with fresh cilantro leaves if desired.

Per Serving: Calories: 320 Protein: 10g Fat: 6g Salt: 700mg

Chilled Cucumber Dill Soup

Total Servings: 1 serving
Preparation Time: 10 minutes
Time to Serve: Chilled (30 minutes or longer)

Ingredients:
- 1 cup diced cucumber (peeled or unpeeled)
- 1/4 cup diced onion
- 1/4 cup fresh dill leaves
- 1 clove garlic, minced
- 1/2 cup unsweetened almond milk
- 1/2 cup low-fat Greek yogurt
- Salt and pepper to taste
- Fresh dill sprigs for garnish (optional)

Instructions:

1. Prepare Ingredients: In a blender or food processor, combine the diced cucumber, diced onion, fresh dill leaves, minced garlic, unsweetened almond milk, and low-fat Greek yogurt.

2. Blend: Blend the mixture until smooth and creamy.

3. Chill: Transfer the cucumber dill soup to a container and refrigerate for at least 30 minutes before serving. Chilling allows the flavors to meld.

4. Season: Taste the chilled soup and adjust the seasoning with salt and pepper.

5. Serve: Ladle the chilled cucumber dill soup into a bowl. Garnish with fresh dill sprigs if desired.

Per Serving: Calories: 220 Protein: 12g Fat: 5g Salt: 600mg

Creamy Sweet Potato Soup

Total Servings: 1 serving
Preparation Time: 10 minutes
Time to Cook: 30 minutes

Ingredients
- 1 medium-sized sweet potato, peeled and diced
- 1/2 small onion, chopped
- 1 garlic clove, minced
- 1/2 teaspoon turmeric powder
- 1/2 teaspoon ginger powder
- 1 cup low-sodium vegetable broth
- 1/4 cup coconut milk (unsweetened)
- Salt and pepper to taste

Instructions

1. In a medium-sized saucepan, heat a little olive oil over medium heat. Add the chopped onions and garlic, and sauté until translucent, about 2-3 minutes.

2. Stir in the turmeric and ginger powder. Cook for an additional minute to release their flavors.

3. Add the diced sweet potato and vegetable broth to the saucepan. Bring to a boil, reduce the heat to low, cover, and simmer for 20-25 minutes or until the sweet potatoes are tender.

4. Use an immersion blender or transfer the soup to puree until smooth.

5. Return the soup to the saucepan, and stir in the coconut milk. Heat gently, but do not bring to a boil.

6. Season with salt and pepper to taste.

7. Serve hot, garnished with a drizzle of coconut milk or a sprinkle of fresh herbs if desired.

Per Serving Calories: 250 Protein: 3g Fat: 10g Salt: 400mg

Lemon Herb Quinoa Soup

Total Servings: 1 serving
Preparation Time: 15 minutes
Time to Cook: 25 minutes

Ingredients

- 1/4 cup quinoa, rinsed and drained
- 1 cup low-sodium vegetable broth
- 1 small carrot, diced
- 1/2 celery stalk, diced
- 1/4 cup frozen peas
- 1/2 lemon, juiced and zested
- 1 teaspoon fresh thyme leaves
- Salt and pepper to taste

Instructions

1. In a saucepan, combine the quinoa and vegetable broth. Bring to a boil, then reduce heat to low, cover, and simmer for 10 minutes.

2. Add the diced carrot, celery, and frozen peas to the saucepan. Continue simmering for 10-15 minutes or until the quinoa and vegetables are tender.

3. Stir in the lemon juice, zest, and fresh thyme leaves. Cook for an additional 2 minutes to incorporate the flavors.

4. Season with salt and pepper to taste.

5. Serve hot.

Per Serving Calories: 280 Protein: 9g Fat: 2g Salt: 450mg

Roasted Beet Orange Soup

Total Servings: 1 serving
Preparation Time: 15 minutes
Time to Cook: 40 minutes

Ingredients

- 1 medium-sized beet, peeled and diced
- 1 small orange, peeled and segmented
- 1/2 small onion, chopped
- 1 garlic clove, minced
- 1 cup low-sodium vegetable broth
- 1 tablespoon olive oil
- Salt and pepper to taste

Instructions

1. Preheat your oven to 400°F (200°C).

2. Toss the diced beet with olive oil, salt, and pepper on a baking sheet. Roast for 30-35 minutes until the beet is tender and slightly caramelized.

3. In a saucepan, heat a little olive oil over medium heat. Add the chopped onion and garlic, and sauté until translucent, about 2-3 minutes.

4. Add the roasted beet, orange segments, and vegetable broth to the saucepan. Bring to a boil, reduce the heat to low, cover, and simmer for 10 minutes.

5. Use an immersion blender or transfer the soup to puree until smooth.

6. Return the soup to the saucepan and heat gently, but do not bring it to a boil.

7. Season with salt and pepper to taste.

8. Serve hot.

Per Serving Calories: 220 Protein: 4g Fat: 7g Salt: 390mg

Spiced Parsnip Coconut Soup

Total Servings: 1 serving
Preparation Time: 15 minutes
Time to Cook: 25 minutes

Ingredients

- 1 medium-sized parsnip, peeled and diced
- 1/2 small onion, chopped
- 1 garlic clove, minced
- 1/2 teaspoon ground cumin
- 1/2 teaspoon ground coriander
- 1/4 teaspoon cayenne pepper (adjust to taste)
- 1 cup low-sodium vegetable broth
- 1/2 cup light coconut milk
- Salt and pepper to taste

Instructions

1. In a medium-sized saucepan, heat a little olive oil over medium heat. Add the chopped onions and garlic, and sauté until translucent, about 2-3 minutes.

2. Stir in the ground cumin, ground coriander, and cayenne pepper. Cook for an additional minute to release their flavors.

3. Add the diced parsnip and vegetable broth to the saucepan. Bring to a boil, then reduce the heat to low, cover, and simmer for 15-20 minutes or until the parsnips are tender.

4. Use an immersion blender or transfer the soup to puree until smooth.

5. Return the soup to the saucepan, and stir in the coconut milk. Heat gently, but do not bring to a boil.

6. Season with salt and pepper to taste.

7. If desired, serve hot, garnished with a sprinkle of ground cayenne pepper or fresh herbs.

Per Serving Calories: 250 Protein: 3 Fat: 12g Salt: 400mg

Creamy Spinach Walnut Soup

Total Servings: 1 serving
Preparation Time: 10 minutes
Time to Cook: 20 minutes

Ingredients

- 1 cup fresh spinach leaves
- 1/4 cup walnuts
- 1/2 small onion, chopped
- 1 garlic clove, minced

- 1 cup low-sodium vegetable broth
- 1/4 cup plain Greek yogurt (unsweetened)
- 1 tablespoon olive oil
- Salt and pepper to taste

Instructions

1. In a small skillet, heat the olive oil over medium heat. Add the chopped onions and garlic, and sauté until translucent, about 2-3 minutes. Remove from heat and set aside.

2. In a separate dry skillet, lightly toast the walnuts over medium heat for 2-3 minutes until they become fragrant. Be careful not to burn them.

3. Combine the fresh spinach, toasted walnuts, sautéed onions and garlic, and vegetable broth in a blender. Blend until smooth.'

4. Pour the mixture back into the skillet and gently heat over low-medium heat.

5. Stir in the Greek yogurt and continue to heat for 3-4 minutes, careful not to boil.

6. Season with salt and pepper to taste.

7. Serve hot, garnished with a sprinkle of crushed walnuts or a drizzle of olive oil if desired.

Per Serving Calories: 280 Protein: 9g Fat: 18g Salt: 400mg

Cajun Red Lentil Soup

Total Servings: 1 serving
Preparation Time: 10 minutes
Time to Cook: 25 minutes

Ingredients

- 1/2 cup red lentils, rinsed and drained
- 1/2 small onion, chopped
- 1 celery stalk, chopped
- 1/2 red bell pepper, diced
- 1 garlic clove, minced
- 1 teaspoon Cajun seasoning (adjust to taste)
- 2 cups low-sodium vegetable broth
- 1 tablespoon olive oil
- Salt and pepper to taste

Instructions

1. In a medium-sized saucepan, heat the olive oil over medium heat. Add the chopped onions, celery, red bell pepper, and garlic. Sauté until the vegetables are softened, about 5-7 minutes.

2. Stir in the Cajun seasoning and cook for another minute to release the flavors.

3. Add the red lentils and vegetable broth to the saucepan. Bring to a boil, then reduce the heat to low, cover, and simmer for 15-20 minutes until the lentils are tender and the soup has thickened.

4. Use an immersion blender or transfer the soup to puree

until smooth.

5. Return the soup to the saucepan and heat gently, but do not bring it to a boil.

6. Season with salt and pepper to taste.

7. If desired, serve hot, garnished with a sprinkle of Cajun seasoning or fresh herbs.

Per Serving Calories: 320 Protein: 15g Fat: 6g Salt: 450mg

Vegan Tomato Basil Bisque

Total Servings: 1 serving
Preparation Time: 15 minutes
Time to Cook: 30 minutes

Ingredients

- 1 cup canned crushed tomatoes
- 1/2 small onion, chopped
- 1 garlic clove, minced
- 1/2 teaspoon dried basil
- 1/4 teaspoon dried oregano
- 1 cup unsweetened almond milk (or other plant-based milk)
- 1 tablespoon nutritional yeast (optional)
- 1 tablespoon olive oil
- Salt and pepper to taste

Instructions

1. In a medium-sized saucepan, heat the olive oil over medium heat. Add the chopped onions and garlic. Sauté until the onions are translucent, about 2-3 minutes.

2. Stir in the dried basil and oregano, and cook for another minute to release their flavors.

3. Add the canned crushed tomatoes to the saucepan. Simmer for 10-15 minutes, stirring occasionally.

4. Pour in the unsweetened almond milk and nutritional yeast (if using). Continue to simmer for an additional 5-10 minutes, allowing the flavors to meld together.

5. Season with salt and pepper to taste.

6. Serve hot.

Per Serving Calories: 180 Protein: 4g Fat: 10g Salt: 400mg

Chapter 8: Smoothies

Tropical Turmeric Smoothie

Total Servings: 1 serving
Preparation Time: 5 minutes
Time to Cook: None

Ingredients
- 1/2 cup frozen pineapple chunks
- 1/2 cup frozen mango chunks
- 1 ripe banana
- 1/2 teaspoon ground turmeric
- 1/2 teaspoon fresh ginger, grated
- 1 cup unsweetened almond milk (or other plant-based milk)
- 1 tablespoon chia seeds (optional for added texture and nutrition)

Instructions

1. Combine the frozen pineapple chunks, frozen mango chunks, ripe banana, ground turmeric, and grated fresh ginger in a blender.

2. Pour in the unsweetened almond milk.

3. Add chia seeds to the blender if you d like a thicker texture and additional nutritional benefits.

4. Blend until smooth and creamy.

5. Pour into a glass and serve immediately.

Per Serving Calories: 260 Protein: 3g Fat: 4g Salt: 150mg

Berry Chia Blast

Total Servings: 1 serving
Preparation Time: 5 minutes
Time to Cook: None

Ingredients
- 1/2 cup mixed berries (strawberries, blueberries, raspberries)
- 1 tablespoon chia seeds
- 1/2 ripe banana
- 1 cup unsweetened coconut milk (or other plant-based milk)
- 1/2 teaspoon honey (optional for added sweetness)

Instructions

6. Combine the mixed berries, chia seeds, and half a ripe banana in a blender.

7. Pour in the unsweetened coconut milk.

8. If you prefer a sweeter taste, add honey to the blender.

9. Blend until the mixture is smooth and the chia seeds are well incorporate

10. Pour into a glass and serve immediately.

Per Serving Calories: 230 Protein: 3g Fat: 8g Salt: 50mg

Pineapple Spinach Green Smoothie

Total Servings: 1 serving
Preparation Time: 5 minutes
Time to Cook: None

Ingredients
- 1 cup fresh spinach leaves
- 1/2 cup frozen pineapple chunks
- 1/2 ripe banana
- 1/2 cup unsweetened coconut water (or other plant-based milk)
- 1/2 teaspoon spirulina powder (optional, for added nutrients)

Instructions

1. Add the fresh spinach leaves, frozen pineapple chunks, and half a ripe banana in a blender.

2. Pour in the unsweetened coconut water.

3. If you want to boost the nutritional content, add spirulina powder to the blender.

4. Blend until smooth and creamy.

5. Pour into a glass and serve immediately.

Per Serving Calories: 190 Protein: 2g Fat: 1g Salt: 60mg

Mango Coconut Shake

Total Servings: 1 serving
Preparation Time: 5 minutes
Time to Cook: None

Ingredients
- 1 ripe mango, peeled and pitted
- 1/2 cup coconut milk (unsweetened)
- 1/2 cup plain Greek yogurt (unsweetened)
- 1 tablespoon honey (optional for added sweetness)
- 1/2 teaspoon ground turmeric
- Ice cubes (optional for a colder shake)

Instructions

1. Combine the ripe mango, coconut milk, and plain Greek yogurt in a blender.

2. Add honey for added sweetness, if desired.

3. Sprinkle in the ground turmeric.

4. Add a few ice cubes to the blender if you prefer a colder shake.

5. Blend until smooth and creamy.

6. Pour into a glass and serve immediately.

Per Serving Calories: 250 Protein: 5g Fat: 12g Salt: 50mg

Strawberry Flax Delight

Total Servings: 1 serving
Preparation Time: 5 minutes
Time to Cook: None

Ingredients

- 1 cup fresh strawberries
- 1 tablespoon ground flaxseeds
- 1/2 cup almond milk (unsweetened)
- 1/2 ripe banana
- 1/2 teaspoon vanilla extract
- 1/2 teaspoon honey (optional for added sweetness)
- Ice cubes (optional for a colder shake)

Instructions

1. In a blender, add the fresh strawberries and ground flaxseeds.

2. Pour in the almond milk.

3. Add the ripe banana and vanilla extract.

4. If you prefer a sweeter taste, add honey to the blender.

5. For a colder shake, add some ice cubes.

6. Blend until smooth and creamy.

7. Pour into a glass and serve immediately.

Per Serving Calories: 220 Protein: 4g Fat: 6g Salt: 60mg

Blueberry Almond Bliss

Total Servings: 1 serving
Preparation Time: 5 minutes
Time to Cook: None

Ingredients

- 1/2 cup blueberries (fresh or frozen)
- 1/4 cup almonds
- 1/2 cup almond milk (unsweetened)
- 1/2 ripe banana
- 1/2 teaspoon cinnamon
- 1/2 teaspoon honey (optional for added sweetness)
- Ice cubes (optional for a colder shake)

Instructions

1. In a blender, combine the blueberries and almonds.

2. Pour in the almond milk.

3. Add the ripe banana and a sprinkle of cinnamon.

4. If you'd like a touch of sweetness, add honey to the

blender.

5. For a colder shake, include some ice cubes.

6. Blend until smooth and creamy.

7. Pour into a glass and serve immediately.

Per Serving Calories: 280 Protein: 7g Fat: 16g Salt: 60mg

Peach Ginger Zing

Total Servings: 1 serving
Preparation Time: 5 minutes
Time to Cook: None

Ingredients

- 1 ripe peach, pitted and sliced
- 1/2-inch piece of fresh ginger, peeled and grated
- 1/2 cup plain Greek yogurt (unsweetened)
- 1/2 cup unsweetened almond milk (or other plant-based milk)
- 1 tablespoon honey (optional for added sweetness)
- Ice cubes (optional for a colder shake)

Instructions

1. In a blender, combine the sliced ripe peach and grated fresh ginger.

2. Add plain Greek yogurt and unsweetened almond milk.

3. If you prefer a sweeter taste, add honey to the blender.

4. For a colder shake, include some ice cubes.

5. Blend until smooth and creamy.

6. Pour into a glass and serve immediately.

Per Serving Calories: 180 Protein: 8g Fat: 5g Salt: 75mg

Avocado Kale Power

Total Servings: 1 serving
Preparation Time: 5 minutes
Time to Cook: None

Ingredients

- 1/2 ripe avocado, peeled and pitted
- 1 cup fresh kale leaves, stems removed
- 1/2 cup unsweetened coconut water (or other plant-based milk)
- 1/2 lemon, juiced
- 1/2 teaspoon spirulina powder (optional, for added nutrients)
- 1/2 teaspoon honey (optional for added sweetness)
- Ice cubes (optional for a colder shake)

Instructions

1. In a blender, combine the ripe avocado and fresh kale leaves.

2. Pour in the unsweetened coconut water.

3. Squeeze the juice from half a lemon into the blender.

4. Add spirulina powder for extra nutrients and honey for

sweetness if desired.

5. For a colder shake, include some ice cubes.

6. Blend until smooth and creamy.

7. Pour into a glass and serve immediately.

Per Serving Calories: 250 Protein: 5g Fat: 15g Salt: 60mg

Cucumber Mint Refresh

Total Servings: 1 serving
Preparation Time: 5 minutes
Time to Cook: None

Ingredients
- 1/2 cucumber, peeled and sliced
- 5-6 fresh mint leaves
- 1/2 cup plain Greek yogurt (unsweetened)
- 1/2 cup unsweetened coconut water (or other plant-based milk)
- 1/2 lime, juiced
- 1/2 teaspoon honey (optional for added sweetness)
- Ice cubes (optional for a colder shake)

Instructions

1. In a blender, combine the sliced cucumber and fresh mint leaves.

2. Add plain Greek yogurt and unsweetened coconut water.

3. Squeeze the juice from half a lime into the blender.

4. Include honey for desired sweetness and ice cubes for a colder shake.

5. Blend until smooth and creamy.

6. Pour into a glass and serve immediately.

Per Serving Calories: 180 Protein: 8g Fat: 5g Salt: 80mg

Raspberry Turmeric Elixir

Total Servings: 1 serving
Preparation Time: 5 minutes
Time to Cook: None

Ingredients
- 1 cup fresh raspberries
- 1/2 teaspoon ground turmeric
- 1/2 teaspoon fresh ginger, grated
- 1/2 cup unsweetened almond milk (or other plant-based milk)
- 1 tablespoon honey (optional for added sweetness)
- 1/2 lemon, juiced
- Ice cubes (optional for a colder elixir)

Instructions

1. Combine the fresh raspberries, ground turmeric, and grated ginger in a blender.

2. Pour in the unsweetened almond milk.

3. Add honey for sweetness if desired.

4. Squeeze the juice from half a lemon into the blender.

5. For a colder elixir, include some ice cubes.

6. Blend until smooth and well combined.

7. Pour into a glass and serve immediately.

Per Serving Calories: 150 Protein: 2g Fat: 2g Salt: 60mg

Banana Spinach Creamsicle

Total Servings: 1 serving
Preparation Time: 5 minutes
Time to Cook: None

Ingredients
- 1 ripe banana
- 1 cup fresh spinach leaves
- 1/2 cup plain Greek yogurt (unsweetened)
- 1/2 cup unsweetened orange juice
- 1/2 teaspoon vanilla extract
- 1/2 teaspoon honey (optional for added sweetness)
- Ice cubes (optional for a colder elixir)

Instructions

1. In a blender, combine the ripe banana and fresh spinach leaves.

2. Pour in plain Greek yogurt and unsweetened orange juice.

3. Add vanilla extract for flavor and honey for sweetness if desired.

4. For a colder elixir, include some ice cubes.

5. Blend until smooth and creamy.

6. Pour into a glass and serve immediately.

Per Serving Calories: 230 Protein: 9g Fat: 2g Salt: 75mg

Cherry Almond Antioxidant

Total Servings: 1 serving
Preparation Time: 5 minutes
Time to Cook: None

Ingredients
- 1/2 cup fresh or frozen cherries
- 1/4 cup almonds
- 1/2 cup unsweetened almond milk (or other plant-based milk)
- 1/2 teaspoon cinnamon
- 1/2 teaspoon honey (optional for added sweetness)
- Ice cubes (optional for a colder elixir)

Instructions

1. In a blender, combine the fresh or frozen cherries and almonds.

2. Pour in the unsweetened almond milk.

3. Add cinnamon for flavor and honey for sweetness if desired.

4. For a colder elixir, include some ice cubes.

5. Blend until smooth and well combined.

6. Pour into a glass and serve immediately.

Per Serving Calories: 280 Protein: 7g Fat: 15g Salt: 60mg

Minty Watermelon Cooler

Total Servings: 1 serving
Preparation Time: 5 minutes
Time to Cook: None

Ingredients
- 1 cup fresh watermelon chunks
- 5-6 fresh mint leaves
- 1/2 lime, juiced
- 1/2 cup coconut water (unsweetened)
- 1/2 teaspoon honey (optional for added sweetness)
- Ice cubes (optional, for a colder cooler)
- Fresh mint sprig for garnish (optional)

Instructions

1. In a blender, combine the fresh watermelon chunks and fresh mint leaves.

2. Squeeze the juice from half a lime into the blender.

3. Pour in the unsweetened coconut water.

4. Add honey for sweetness if desired.

5. For a colder cooler, include some ice cubes.

6. Blend until smooth and well combined.

7. If desired, pour into a glass, garnish with a fresh mint sprig, and serve immediately.

Per Serving Calories: 90 Protein: 1g Fat: 0.5g Salt: 100mg

Kiwi Avocado Fusion

Total Servings: 1 serving
Preparation Time: 5 minutes
Time to Cook: None

Ingredients
- 2 ripe kiwis, peeled and sliced
- 1/2 ripe avocado, peeled and pitted
- 1/2 cup unsweetened almond milk (or other plant-based milk)
- 1/2 teaspoon honey (optional for added sweetness)
- Ice cubes (optional for a colder fusion)
- Fresh kiwi slice for garnish (optional)

Instructions

1. In a blender, combine the ripe kiwis and ripe avocado.

2. Pour in the unsweetened almond milk.

3. Add honey for sweetness if desired.

4. For a colder fusion, include some ice cubes.

5. Blend until smooth and creamy.

6. If desired, pour into a glass, garnish with a fresh kiwi slice, and serve immediately.

Per Serving Calories: 230 Protein: 3g Fat: 13g Salt: 50mg

Golden Mango Tango

Total Servings: 1 serving
Preparation Time: 5 minutes
Time to Cook: None

Ingredients
- 1 ripe mango, peeled and pitted
- 1/2 teaspoon ground turmeric
- 1/2 teaspoon fresh ginger, grated
- 1/2 cup unsweetened coconut milk (or other plant-based milk)
- 1/2 teaspoon honey (optional for added sweetness)
- Ice cubes (optional for a colder tango)
- Fresh mango slice for garnish (optional)

Instructions

1. Combine the ripe mango, ground turmeric, and grated fresh ginger in a blender.

2. Pour in the unsweetened coconut milk.

3. Add honey for sweetness if desired.

4. For a colder tango, include some ice cubes.

5. Blend until smooth and well combined.

6. If desired, pour into a glass, garnish with a fresh mango slice, and serve immediately.

Per Serving Calories: 250 Protein: 3g Fat: 6g Salt: 40mg

Spiced Carrot Orange

Total Servings: 1 serving
Preparation Time: 5 minutes
Time to Cook: None

Ingredients
- 1 large carrot, peeled and chopped
- 1 large orange, peeled and segmented
- 1/2 teaspoon ground cinnamon
- 1/4 teaspoon ground turmeric
- 1/2 cup unsweetened almond milk (or other plant-based milk)
- 1/2 teaspoon honey (optional for added sweetness)
- Ice cubes (optional for a colder drink)

Instructions

1. In a blender, combine the chopped carrot and segmented orange.

2. Sprinkle in the ground cinnamon and ground turmeric.

3. Pour in the unsweetened almond milk.

4. Add honey for sweetness if desired.

5. If you prefer a colder drink, include some ice cubes.

6. Blend until smooth and well combined.

7. Pour into a glass and serve immediately.

Per Serving Calories: 120 Protein: 2g Fat: 2g Salt: 90mg

Pineapple Basil Breeze

Total Servings: 1 serving
Preparation Time: 5 minutes
Time to Cook: None

Ingredients
- 1 cup fresh pineapple chunks
- 5-6 fresh basil leaves
- 1/2 cup unsweetened coconut water (or other plant-based milk)
- 1/2 lime, juiced
- 1/2 teaspoon honey (optional, for added sweetness)
- Ice cubes (optional for a colder drink)
- Fresh basil sprig for garnish (optional)

Instructions

1. In a blender, combine the fresh pineapple chunks and fresh basil leaves.

2. Squeeze the juice from half a lime into the blender.

3. Pour in the unsweetened coconut water.

4. Add honey for sweetness if desired.

5. For a colder drink, include some ice cubes.

6. Blend until smooth and well combined.

7. If desired, pour into a glass, garnish with a fresh basil sprig, and serve immediately.

Per Serving Calories: 130 Protein: 1g Fat: 1g Salt: 60mg

Pomegranate Beet Elixir

Total Servings: 1 serving
Preparation Time: 5 minutes
Time to Cook: None

Ingredients
- 1/2 medium-sized beetroot, peeled and chopped
- 1/2 cup pomegranate seeds
- 1/2 cup unsweetened almond milk (or other plant-based milk)
- 1/2 lemon, juiced
- 1/2 teaspoon honey (optional for added sweetness)
- Ice cubes (optional for a colder elixir)
- Fresh pomegranate arils for garnish (optional)

Instructions

1. In a blender, combine the chopped beetroot and pomegranate seeds.

2. Squeeze the juice from half a lemon into the blender.

3. Pour in the unsweetened almond milk.

4. Add honey for sweetness if desired.

5. For a colder elixir, include some ice cubes.

6. Blend until smooth and well combined.

7. If desired, pour into a glass, garnish with fresh pomegranate arils, and serve immediately.

Per Serving Calories: 160 Protein: 2g Fat: 2g Salt: 90mg

Cranberry Cinnamon Spice

Total Servings: 1 serving
Preparation Time: 5 minutes
Time to Cook: None

Ingredients
- 1/2 cup fresh cranberries
- 1/2 teaspoon ground cinnamon
- 1/4 teaspoon ground nutmeg
- 1/2 cup unsweetened almond milk (or other plant-based milk)
- 1/2 teaspoon honey (optional for added sweetness)
- Ice cubes (optional for a colder drink)
- Fresh cranberry for garnish (optional)

Instructions

1. Combine the fresh cranberries, ground cinnamon, and ground nutmeg in a blender.

2. Pour in the unsweetened almond milk.

3. Add honey for sweetness if desired.

4. For a colder drink, include some ice cubes.

5. Blend until smooth and well combined.

6. Pour into a glass, garnish with a fresh cranberry if desired, and serve immediately.

Per Serving Calories: 90 Protein: 1g Fat: 1g Salt: 70mg

Coconut Papaya Dream

Total Servings: 1 serving
Preparation Time: 5 minutes
Time to Cook: None

Ingredients
- 1/2 cup ripe papaya chunks
- 1/2 cup unsweetened coconut milk
- 1/2 teaspoon honey (optional for added sweetness)
- 1/2 teaspoon vanilla extract
- Ice cubes (optional for a colder drink)
- Fresh papaya slice for garnish (optional)

- Unsweetened shredded coconut for garnish (optional)

Instructions

1. Combine the ripe papaya chunks, unsweetened coconut milk, honey, and vanilla extract in a blender.

2. For a colder drink, include some ice cubes.

3. Blend until smooth and well combined.

4. Pour into a glass.

5. Garnish with a fresh papaya slice and a sprinkle of unsweetened shredded coconut if desired.

6. Serve immediately.

Per Serving Calories: 180 Protein: 1g Fat: 10g Salt: 10mg

Chapter 9: Desserts

Mango Turmeric Sorbet

Total Servings: 1 serving
Preparation Time: 10 minutes
Time to Cook: 0 minutes

Ingredients

- 1 ripe mango, peeled, pitted, and diced
- 1/2 teaspoon ground turmeric
- 1 tablespoon honey (optional for added sweetness)
- 1/4 cup unsweetened coconut milk (or other plant-based milk)
- Juice of 1/2 lime
- Fresh mint leaves for garnish (optional)

Instructions

1. Place the diced ripe mango in a blender.
2. Add ground turmeric and honey (if desired).
3. Squeeze the juice of half a lime into the blender.
4. Pour in the unsweetened coconut milk.
5. Blend until smooth and creamy.
6. Transfer the mixture to an airtight container and freeze for about 3-4 hours or until it reaches a sorbet-like consistency.
7. If desired, serve the mango turmeric sorbet in a bowl garnished with fresh mint leaves.

Per Serving Calories: 220 Protein: 2g Fat: 4g Salt: 10mg

Berry Seed Parfait

Total Servings: 1 serving
Preparation Time: 10 minutes
Time to Cook: 0 minutes

Ingredients

- 1/2 cup mixed berries (strawberries, blueberries, raspberries)
- 1/4 cup Greek yogurt (unsweetened)
- 1 tablespoon chia seeds
- 1/4 cup granola (unsweetened)
- 1/2 teaspoon honey (optional for added sweetness)
- Fresh berries for garnish (optional)

Instructions

1. In a bowl or glass, start with a layer of mixed berries.
2. Add a layer of Greek yogurt.
3. Sprinkle chia seeds over the yogurt layer.
4. Add a layer of granola.

5. Drizzle honey over the top for sweetness (if desired).
6. Repeat the layers until your glass is filled.
7. Garnish with fresh berries if desired.

Per Serving Calories: 300 Protein: 10g Fat: 10g Salt: 40mg

Avocado Choc Mousse

Total Servings: 1 serving
Preparation Time: 10 minutes
Time to Cook: 0 minutes

Ingredients

- 1 ripe avocado, peeled and pitted
- 2 tablespoons unsweetened cocoa powder
- 1 tablespoon honey (optional for added sweetness)
- 1/4 teaspoon vanilla extract
- 2 tablespoons unsweetened almond milk (or other plant-based milk)
- Fresh berries for garnish (optional)

Instructions

1. Combine the ripe avocado, unsweetened cocoa powder, honey (if desired), and vanilla extract in a blender.
2. Pour in the unsweetened almond milk.
3. Blend until smooth and creamy.
4. Transfer the avocado chocolate mousse into a bowl or glass.
5. Garnish with fresh berries if desired.
6. Serve immediately, or refrigerate for a chilled treat.

Per Serving Calories: 280 Protein: 4g Fat: 20g Salt: 10mg

Cinnamon Walnut Apples

Total Servings: 1 serving
Preparation Time: 10 minutes
Time to Cook: 5 minutes

Ingredients

- 1 apple, cored and sliced
- 1/2 teaspoon ground cinnamon
- 1 tablespoon chopped walnuts
- 1 teaspoon honey (optional for added sweetness)
- 1/4 cup Greek yogurt (unsweetened)
- Fresh mint leaves for garnish (optional)
- Lemon zest for garnish (optional)

Instructions

1. In a pan over medium heat, add the sliced apples.

2. Sprinkle ground cinnamon over the apples.

3. Sauté for about 5 minutes or until the apples are tender.

4. Transfer the cooked apples to a serving dish.

5. Sprinkle chopped walnuts over the apples.

6. Drizzle honey for added sweetness (if desired).

7. Serve the warm cinnamon walnut apples with a side of Greek yogurt and garnish with fresh mint leaves and lemon zest if desired.

Per Serving Calories: 250 Protein: 7g Fat: 10g Salt: 10mg

Blueberry Coconut Pops

Total Servings: 1 serving
Preparation Time: 10 minutes
Time to Cook: 4 hours (freezing time)

Ingredients

- 1/2 cup blueberries (fresh or frozen)
- 1/2 cup coconut milk (unsweetened)
- 1/2 teaspoon honey (optional for added sweetness)
- 1/4 teaspoon vanilla extract
- 1 tablespoon shredded coconut
- Popsicle mold and sticks

Instructions

1. Combine the blueberries, coconut milk, honey (if desired), and vanilla extract in a blender.

2. Blend until smooth.

3. Pour the mixture into popsicle molds.

4. Insert popsicle sticks into the molds.

5. Sprinkle shredded coconut over the top of each mold.

6. Freeze for at least 4 hours or until the popsicles are solid.

7. Remove from the molds and enjoy these refreshing blueberry coconut pops.

Per Serving Calories: 180 Protein: 1g Fat: 11g Salt: 10mg

Banana Almond Ice Cream

Total Servings: 1 serving
Preparation Time: 5 minutes
Time to Cook: 0 minutes

Ingredients

- 1 ripe banana, peeled and sliced
- 1/4 cup almond butter (unsweetened)
- 1/2 teaspoon vanilla extract
- 1/4 teaspoon ground cinnamon
- 1/4 cup almond milk (unsweetened)

- 1 teaspoon honey (optional for added sweetness)
- Sliced almonds for garnish (optional)

Instructions

1. Combine the sliced ripe banana, almond butter, vanilla extract, and ground cinnamon in a blender.

2. Pour in the unsweetened almond milk.

3. Add honey for sweetness if desired.

4. Blend until smooth and creamy.

5. Transfer the banana almond ice cream into a bowl.

6. Garnish with sliced almonds if desired.

7. Serve immediately or freeze for a firmer texture.

Per Serving Calories: 380 Protein: 8g Fat: 28g Salt: 10mg

Lemon Poppy Seed Bites

Total Servings: 1 serving
Preparation Time: 10 minutes
Time to Cook: 0 minutes

Ingredients

- 1/2 cup rolled oats
- 2 tablespoons almond butter (unsweetened)
- 1 tablespoon honey (or maple syrup for a vegan option)
- 1/2 lemon, zest and juice
- 1/2 teaspoon poppy seeds
- A pinch of sea salt
- Unsweetened shredded coconut for rolling (optional)

Instructions

1. Combine rolled oats, almond butter, honey (or maple syrup), lemon zest, lemon juice, poppy seeds, and a pinch of sea salt in a bowl.

2. Mix the ingredients until well combined.

3. Take small portions of the mixture and roll them into bite-sized balls.

4. If desired, roll the bites in unsweetened shredded coconut for an extra layer of flavor.

5. Place the bites on a plate and refrigerate for at least 30 minutes to set.

6. Once firm, your Lemon Poppy Seed Bites are ready to enjoy as a snack or dessert.

Per Serving Calories: 290 Protein: 7g Fat: 12g Salt: 60mg

Pineapple Turmeric FroYo

Total Servings: 1 serving
Preparation Time: 5 minutes
Time to Cook: 4 hours (freezing time)

Ingredients

- 1/2 cup frozen pineapple chunks
- 1/2 teaspoon ground turmeric
- 1/4 cup Greek yogurt (unsweetened)
- 1/2 teaspoon honey (optional for added sweetness)
- 1/4 teaspoon vanilla extract
- Fresh mint leaves for garnish (optional)

Instructions

1. In a blender, combine frozen pineapple chunks, ground turmeric, Greek yogurt, honey (if desired), and vanilla extract.

2. Blend until smooth.

3. Transfer the mixture into a container suitable for freezing.

4. Freeze for at least 4 hours until it reaches a firm, frozen yogurt consistency.

5. Scoop out your Pineapple Turmeric FroYo and garnish with fresh mint leaves if desired.

6. Serve immediately.

Per Serving Calories: 180 Protein: 7g Fat: 2g Salt: 40mg

Peach Almond Crisp

Total Servings: 1 serving
Preparation Time: 10 minutes
Time to Cook: 30 minutes

Ingredients

- 1 ripe peach, sliced
- 1/4 cup rolled oats
- 1 tablespoon almond meal (ground almonds)
- 1/2 teaspoon ground cinnamon
- 1/2 teaspoon honey (or maple syrup for a vegan option)
- 1/4 teaspoon vanilla extract
- A pinch of sea salt

Instructions

1. Preheat your oven to 350°F (175°C).

2. Combine sliced ripe peach, rolled oats, almond meal, ground cinnamon, honey (or maple syrup), vanilla extract, and a pinch of sea salt.

3. Mix until the ingredients are well combined, and the peaches are coated.

4. Transfer the mixture to an oven-safe dish.

5. Bake for approximately 30 minutes or until the top is golden brown and the peaches are tender.

6. Allow it to cool for a few minutes, then enjoy your warm Peach Almond Crisp.

Per Serving Calories: 280 Protein: 7g Fat: 8g Salt: 80mg

Strawberry Basil Sorbet

Total Servings: 1 serving
Preparation Time: 10 minutes
Time to Cook: 0 minutes

Ingredients

- 1 cup fresh strawberries, hulled and halved
- 4-5 fresh basil leaves
- 1/2 lemon, juiced
- 1/2 teaspoon honey (optional for added sweetness)
- Ice cubes (optional for a colder sorbet)
- Fresh basil sprig for garnish (optional)

Instructions

1. In a blender, combine the fresh strawberries and fresh basil leaves.

2. Squeeze the juice from half a lemon into the blender.

3. Add honey for sweetness if desired.

4. For a colder sorbet, include some ice cubes.

5. Blend until smooth and well combined.

6. Transfer the sorbet into a bowl.

7. Garnish with a fresh basil sprig if desired.

8. Serve immediately.

Per Serving Calories: 80 Protein: 1g Fat: 0.5g Salt: 0mg

Choc Avocado Truffles

Total Servings: 1 serving
Preparation Time: 15 minutes
Time to Cook: 0 minutes

Ingredients

- 1/2 ripe avocado, peeled and pitted
- 1 tablespoon unsweetened cocoa powder
- 1 tablespoon honey (or maple syrup for a vegan option)
- 1/4 teaspoon vanilla extract
- A pinch of sea salt
- Unsweetened shredded coconut or crushed nuts for coating (optional)

Instructions

1. In a bowl, mash the ripe avocado until smooth.

2. Add unsweetened cocoa powder, honey (or maple syrup), vanilla extract, and a pinch of sea salt.

3. Mix until all ingredients are well combined.

4. Refrigerate the mixture for 10-15 minutes to firm it up slightly.

5. Once the mixture is firm enough to handle, roll it into bite-sized truffle balls.

6. Roll the truffles in unsweetened shredded coconut or

crushed nuts for coating if desired.

7. Place the truffles on a plate and refrigerate for 15-20 minutes to set.

8. Your Choc Avocado Truffles are ready to enjoy.

Per Serving Calories: 230 Protein: 2g Fat: 16g Salt: 60mg

Almond Berry Bark

Total Servings: 1 serving
Preparation Time: 10 minutes
Time to Cook: 1 hour (freezing time)

Ingredients

- 1/4 cup mixed berries (strawberries, blueberries, raspberries)
- 1/4 cup almonds, chopped
- 1 tablespoon honey (or maple syrup for a vegan option)
- A pinch of sea salt
- Unsweetened shredded coconut for garnish (optional)

Instructions

1. Line a small tray or dish with parchment paper.

2. Combine mixed berries, chopped almonds, honey (or maple syrup), and a pinch of sea salt in a bowl.

3. Mix until everything is well-coated.

4. Spread the mixture evenly on the parchment paper.

5. If desired, sprinkle unsweetened shredded coconut over the top.

6. Place the tray in the freezer for at least 1 hour or until the bark is completely frozen.

7. Break the Almond Berry Bark into pieces and enjoy.

Per Serving Calories: 270 Protein: 6g Fat: 15g Salt: 60mg

Cardamom Poached Pears

Total Servings: 1 serving
Preparation Time: 10 minutes
Time to Cook: 20 minutes

Ingredients

- 1 ripe pear, peeled and cored
- cup water
- 1/2 teaspoon ground cardamom
- 1 tablespoon honey (optional for added sweetness)
- 1/4 teaspoon vanilla extract
- A pinch of sea salt
- Chopped nuts for garnish (optional)

Instructions

1. Combine water, ground cardamom, honey (if desired), vanilla extract, and a pinch of sea salt in a saucepan.

2. Place the peeled and cored ripe pear into the saucepan.

3. Bring the mixture to a gentle simmer over low heat.

4. Cover and let the pear poach for about 15-20 minutes or until it›s tender when pierced with a fork.

5. Remove the pear from the poaching liquid and let it cool slightly.

6. Slice the poached pear and place it on a plate.

7. Drizzle any remaining poaching liquid over the pear slices.

8. Garnish with chopped nuts if desired.

9. Serve your cardamom-poached pears warm.

Per Serving Calories: 200 Protein: 1g Fat: 0.5g Salt: 60mg

Mint Choc Chip Cream

Total Servings: 1 serving
Preparation Time: 5 minutes
Time to Cook: 0 minutes

Ingredients

- 1/2 cup Greek yogurt (unsweetened)
- 1/4 teaspoon peppermint extract
- 1/2 teaspoon honey (optional for added sweetness)
- 1 tablespoon dark chocolate chips (70% cocoa or higher)
- Fresh mint leaves for garnish (optional)

Instructions

1. In a bowl, combine Greek yogurt, peppermint extract, and honey (if desired).

2. Mix until well combined.

3. Add dark chocolate chips to the mixture and gently fold them in.

4. Transfer the Mint Choc Chip Cream to a serving dish.

5. Garnish with fresh mint leaves if desired.

6. Serve immediately.

Per Serving Calories: 220 Protein: 10g Fat: 10g Salt: 30mg

Stuffed Date Bites

Total Servings: 1 serving
Preparation Time: 10 minutes
Time to Cook: 0 minutes

Ingredients

- 3 Medjool dates, pitted
- 1 teaspoon almond butter (unsweetened)
- 1 teaspoon unsweetened shredded coconut
- 3 whole almonds
- A pinch of sea salt
- Ground cinnamon for garnish (optional)

Instructions

1. Carefully slice each pitted Medjool date along one side to create an opening.

2. Stuff each date with almond butter and a whole almond.

3. Sprinkle unsweetened shredded coconut over the stuffed dates.

4. Add a pinch of sea salt.

5. f desired, dust the dates with ground cinnamon.

6. Arrange the Stuffed Date Bites on a plate.

7. Serve immediately as a delicious and healthy snack.

Per Serving Calories: 180 Protein: 2g Fat: 4g Salt: 0mg

Berry Oat Bars

Total Servings: 1 serving
Preparation Time: 15 minutes
Time to Cook: 25 minutes

Ingredients
- 1/2 cup rolled oats
- 1/4 cup mixed berries (strawberries, blueberries, raspberries)
- 1 tablespoon almond butter (unsweetened)
- 1/2 teaspoon honey (optional for added sweetness)
- 1/4 teaspoon ground cinnamon
- 1/4 teaspoon vanilla extract
- A pinch of sea salt

Instructions

1. Preheat your oven to 350°F (175°C) and line a small baking dish with parchment paper.

2. Combine rolled oats, mixed berries, almond butter, honey (if desired), ground cinnamon, vanilla extract, and a pinch of sea salt in a bowl.

3. Mix until all ingredients are well combined.

4. Transfer the mixture to the lined baking dish and press it down evenly.

5. Bake for about 25 minutes or until the top is golden brown.

6. Remove from the oven and let it cool for a few minutes.

7. Cut the baked mixture into bars or squares.

8. Enjoy your homemade Berry Oat Bars!

Per Serving Calories: 280 Protein: 7g Fat: 10g Salt: 60mg

Pumpkin Spice Bites

Total Servings: 1 serving
Preparation Time: 10 minutes
Time to Cook: 0 minutes

Ingredients
- 1/2 cup canned pumpkin puree (unsweetened)
- 1/4 cup almond meal (ground almonds)
- 1/2 teaspoon pumpkin pie spice

- 1/2 teaspoon honey (optional for added sweetness)
- 1/4 teaspoon vanilla extract
- Unsweetened shredded coconut for coating (optional)
- Pumpkin seeds for garnish (optional)

Instructions

1. Combine canned pumpkin puree, almond meal, pumpkin pie spice, honey (if desired), and vanilla extract.

2. Mix until you have a dough-like consistency.

3. Roll the mixture into bite-sized balls.

4. If desired, roll the balls in unsweetened shredded coconut for coating.

5. Garnish with pumpkin seeds if desired.

6. Your Pumpkin Spice Bites are ready to enjoy as a healthy snack or dessert.

Per Serving Calories: 220 Protein: 7g Fat: 16g Salt: 10mg

Lime Coconut Pudding

Total Servings: 1 serving
Preparation Time: 10 minutes
Time to Cook: 0 minutes

Ingredients
- 1/2 cup Greek yogurt (unsweetened)
- Zest and juice of 1 lime
- 1/2 teaspoon honey (optional for added sweetness)
- 1 tablespoon unsweetened shredded coconut
- Lime zest for garnish (optional)
- Fresh mint leaves for garnish (optional)

Instructions

1. In a bowl, combine Greek yogurt, lime zest, lime juice, and honey (if desired).

2. Mix until all ingredients are well combined.

3. Transfer the Lime Coconut Pudding to a serving dish.

4. Sprinkle unsweetened shredded coconut over the top.

5. If desired, garnish with lime zest and fresh mint leaves.

6. Serve your Lime Coconut Pudding immediately.

Per Serving Calories: 180 Protein: 10g Fat: 8g Salt: 30mg

Cherry Almond Bars

Total Servings: 1 serving
Preparation Time: 15 minutes
Time to Cook: 25 minutes

Ingredients
- 1/2 cup rolled oats
- 1/4 cup dried cherries
- 1 tablespoon almond butter (unsweetened)
- 1/2 teaspoon honey (optional for added sweetness)
- 1/4 teaspoon almond extract

- A pinch of sea salt
- Sliced almonds for garnish (optional)

Instructions

1. Preheat your oven to 350°F (175°C) and line a small baking dish with parchment paper.

2. Combine rolled oats, dried cherries, almond butter, honey (if desired), almond extract, and a pinch of sea salt in a bowl.

3. Mix until all ingredients are well combined.

4. Transfer the mixture to the lined baking dish and press it down evenly.

5. Bake for about 25 minutes or until the top is golden brown.

6. Remove from the oven and let it cool for a few minutes.

7. Cut the baked mixture into bars or squares.

8. Enjoy your homemade Cherry Almond Bars!

Per Serving Calories: 280 Protein: 7g Fat: 10g Salt: 60mg

Berry Chia Pudding

Total Servings: 1 serving
Preparation Time: 10 minutes
Time to Cook: 4 hours (chilling time)

Ingredients
- 1/2 cup mixed berries (strawberries, blueberries, raspberries)
- 2 tablespoons chia seeds
- 1/2 cup unsweetened almond milk (or other plant-based milk)
- 1/2 teaspoon honey (optional for added sweetness)
- 1/4 teaspoon vanilla extract
- Fresh berries for garnish (optional)
- Fresh mint leaves for garnish (optional)

Instructions

1. Combine mixed berries, chia seeds, unsweetened almond milk, honey (if desired), and vanilla extract in a bowl.

2. Mix until well combined.

3. Transfer the mixture into a jar or glass.

4. Cover and refrigerate for at least 4 hours or overnight to allow the chia seeds to absorb the liquid and create a pudding-like texture.

5. Before serving, garnish with fresh berries and fresh mint leaves if desired.

6. Enjoy your Berry Chia Pudding as a healthy and delicious dessert or snack.

Per Serving Calories: 180 Protein: 4g Fat: 9g Salt: 30mg

Matcha Tea Pops

Total Servings: 1 serving
Preparation Time: 10 minutes
Time to Cook: 4 hours (freezing time)

Ingredients
- 1 teaspoon matcha green tea powder
- 1/2 cup coconut milk (unsweetened)
- 1/2 teaspoon honey (optional for added sweetness)
- 1/4 teaspoon vanilla extract
- Matcha green tea leaves for garnish (optional)

Instructions

1. Combine matcha green tea powder, coconut milk, honey (if desired), and vanilla extract in a bowl.

2. Mix until the ingredients are well combined.

3. Pour the mixture into popsicle molds.

4. Insert popsicle sticks into the molds.

5. Freeze for at least 4 hours or until the popsicles are solid.

6. Before serving, garnish with a sprinkle of matcha green tea leaves if desired.

7. Enjoy your refreshing Matcha Tea Pops!

Per Serving Calories: 160 Protein: 2g Fat: 12g Salt: 20mg

Choc Turmeric Bark

Total Servings: 1 serving
Preparation Time: 10 minutes
Time to Cook: 1 hour (freezing time)

Ingredients
- 1 tablespoon unsweetened cocoa powder
- 1/2 teaspoon ground turmeric
- 1 tablespoon honey (or maple syrup for a vegan option)
- 1/4 cup coconut oil (melted)
- A pinch of sea salt
- Chopped nuts (such as almonds or walnuts) for garnish (optional)
- Unsweetened shredded coconut for garnish (optional)

Instructions

1. Combine unsweetened cocoa powder, ground turmeric, honey (or maple syrup), melted coconut oil, and a pinch of sea salt in a bowl.

2. Mix until you have a smooth chocolate mixture.

3. Line a small tray or dish with parchment paper.

4. Pour the chocolate mixture onto the parchment paper and spread it out evenly.

5. If desired, sprinkle chopped nuts and unsweetened shredded coconut over the top for added texture and flavor.

6. Place the tray in the freezer for about 1 hour or until the bark is solid.

7. Remove from the freezer and break the Choc Turmeric Bark into pieces.

8. Enjoy your homemade anti-inflammatory chocolate treat!

Per Serving Calories: 350 Protein: 2g Fat: 32g Salt: 60mg

Lemon Cheesecake Bites

Total Servings: 1 serving
Preparation Time: 15 minutes
Time to Cook: 0 minutes

Ingredients
- 1/2 cup Greek yogurt (unsweetened)
- Zest and juice of 1 lemon
- 1/2 teaspoon honey (optional for added sweetness)
- 1/4 teaspoon vanilla extract
- A pinch of sea salt
- Fresh lemon zest for garnish (optional)
- Fresh berries for garnish (optional)

Instructions

1. In a bowl, combine Greek yogurt, lemon zest, lemon juice, honey (if desired), vanilla extract, and a pinch of sea salt.

2. Mix until all ingredients are well combined.

3. Transfer the Lemon Cheesecake mixture to a serving dish.

4. If desired, garnish with fresh lemon zest and fresh berries.

5. Serve immediately as a delightful and tangy dessert.

Per Serving Calories: 190 Protein: 10g Fat: 4g Salt: 30mg

Pistachio Rice Pudding

Total Servings: 1 serving
Preparation Time: 10 minutes
Time to Cook: 25 minutes

Ingredients
- 1/4 cup brown rice
- 1 cup unsweetened almond milk (or other plant-based milk)
- 1/4 teaspoon ground cinnamon
- 1/4 teaspoon ground cardamom
- 1 tablespoon honey (or maple syrup for a vegan option)
- 1/4 cup unsalted pistachios, chopped
- A pinch of sea salt

Instructions

1. Rinse the brown rice thoroughly under cold water.

2. Combine brown rice, unsweetened almond milk, ground cinnamon, ground cardamom, honey (if desired), and a pinch of sea salt in a saucepan.

3. Bring the mixture to a boil over medium heat.

4. Reduce the heat to low, cover, and let it simmer for about 25 minutes or until the rice is tender and the liquid has been absorbed. Stir occasionally.

5. Remove from heat and let the Pistachio Rice Pudding cool slightly.

6. Transfer to a bowl and sprinkle chopped pistachios over the top.

7. Enjoy your creamy and aromatic Pistachio Rice Pudding.

Per Serving Calories: 380 Protein: 8 Fat: 14g Salt: 60mg

Cranberry Walnut Cookies

Total Servings: 1 serving
Preparation Time: 15 minutes
Time to Cook: 12-15 minutes

Ingredients
- 1/4 cup rolled oats
- 1 tablespoon dried cranberries
- 1 tablespoon chopped walnuts
- 1 tablespoon almond butter (unsweetened)
- 1/2 teaspoon honey (optional for added sweetness)
- A pinch of ground cinnamon
- A pinch of sea salt

Instructions

1. Preheat your oven to 350°F (175°C) and line a baking sheet with parchment paper.

2. Combine rolled oats, dried cranberries, chopped walnuts, almond butter, honey (if desired), ground cinnamon, and a pinch of sea salt.

3. Mix until all ingredients are well combined.

4. Form the mixture into a cookie shape and place it on the prepared baking sheet.

5. Bake for 12-15 minutes or until the edges are golden brown.

6. Remove from the oven and let the Cranberry Walnut Cookies cool for a few minutes.

7. Enjoy your homemade anti-inflammatory cookies!

Per Serving Calories: 230 Protein: 5g Fat: 15g Salt: 90mg

Apricot Energy Balls

Total Servings: 1 serving
Preparation Time: 10 minutes
Time to Cook: 0 minutes

Ingredients
- 3 dried apricots
- 1 tablespoon almond meal (ground almonds
- 1 tablespoon unsweetened shredded coconut
- 1/2 teaspoon honey (optional for added sweetness)
- A pinch of ground ginger
- A pinch of sea salt
- Unsweetened shredded coconut for coating (optional)

Instructions

1. In a food processor, combine dried apricots, almond meal, unsweetened shredded coconut, honey (if desired), ground ginger, and a pinch of sea salt.

2. Process until the mixture comes together into a sticky dough.

3. Roll the dough into bite-sized energy balls.

4. If desired, roll the balls in unsweetened shredded coconut for coating.

5. Your Apricot Energy Balls are ready to enjoy as a nutritious snack.

Per Serving Calories: 180 Protein: 4g Fat: 11g Salt: 10mg

Choc-Dipped Strawberries

Total Servings: 1 serving
Preparation Time: 10 minutes
Time to Cook: 0 minutes

Instructions

1. Wash and dry the fresh strawberries, leaving the stems intact.

2. In a microwave-safe bowl, melt the dark chocolate chips in 20-second intervals until smooth.

3. Dip each strawberry into the melted chocolate, covering about half of the strawberry.

4. Place the chocolate-dipped strawberries on a plate lined with parchment paper.

5. Sprinkle a pinch of sea salt over the chocolate while it's still wet.

6. Let the chocolate harden for a few minutes.

7. Enjoy your Choc-Dipped Strawberries as a delightful treat!

Per Serving Calories: 120 Protein: 1g Fat: 5g Salt: 60mg

Coconut Choc Truffles

Total Servings: 1 serving
Preparation Time: 15 minutes
Time to Cook: 0 minutes

Ingredients

- 2 tablespoons unsweetened shredded coconut
- 1 tablespoon unsweetened cocoa powder
- 1/2 tablespoon coconut oil (melted)
- 1/2 teaspoon honey (optional for added sweetness)
- A pinch of sea salt
- Unsweetened cocoa powder for coating (optional)

Instructions

1. In a bowl, combine unsweetened shredded coconut, unsweetened cocoa powder, melted coconut oil, honey (if desired), and a pinch of sea salt.

2. Mix until you have a dough-like consistency.

3. Roll the mixture into bite-sized truffles.

4. If desired, roll the truffles in unsweetened cocoa powder for coating.

5. Place the Coconut Choc Truffles in the refrigerator for 15 minutes to firm up.

6. Enjoy your homemade anti-inflammatory chocolate truffles!

Per Serving Calories: 200 Protein: 2g Fat: 17g Salt: 60mg

Almond Raspberry Tart

Total Servings: 1 serving
Preparation Time: 15 minutes
Time to Cook: 25 minutes

Ingredients

- 1/4 cup almond meal (ground almonds)
- 1/4 cup fresh raspberries
- 1/2 tablespoon honey (optional for added sweetness)
- 1/4 teaspoon almond extract
- A pinch of sea salt
- Sliced almonds for garnish (optional)

Instructions

1. Preheat your oven to 350°F (175°C) and grease a small tart dish or ramekin.

2. Combine almond meal, fresh raspberries, honey (if desired), almond extract, and a pinch of sea salt.

3. Mix until well combined.

4. Transfer the mixture to the greased tart dish or ramekin.

5. If desired, garnish with sliced almonds for added texture.

6. Bake for about 25 minutes or until the tart is set and the top is lightly golden.

7. Remove from the oven and let it cool for a few minutes.

8. Enjoy your Almond Raspberry Tart as a delicious anti-inflammatory dessert.

Per Serving Calories: 320 Protein: 7g Fat: 21g Salt: 60mg

Cinnamon Peach Roast

Total Servings: 1 serving
Preparation Time: 10 minutes
Time to Cook: 25 minutes

Ingredients

- 1 ripe peach, halved and pitted
- 1/2 teaspoon ground cinnamon
- 1/2 teaspoon honey (optional for added sweetness)
- A pinch of sea salt
- Chopped nuts (such as almonds or walnuts) for garnish (optional)
- Unsweetened yogurt for serving (optional)

Instructions

1. Preheat your oven to 350°F (175°C) and line a small baking dish with parchment paper.

2. Place the halved and pitted ripe peach in the baking dish.

3. Sprinkle ground cinnamon over the peach halves.

4. Drizzle honey (if desired) over the top and add a pinch of sea salt.

5. Bake for about 25 minutes or until the peach is tender and the edges are caramelized.

6. Remove from the oven and let it cool slightly.

7. If desired, garnish with chopped nuts and serve with unsweetened yogurt.

8. Enjoy your warm and fragrant Cinnamon Peach Roast!

Per Serving Calories: 150 Protein: 2g Fat: 5g Salt: 60mg

Chapter 10: Snack and Appetizer

Baked Kale Chips

Total Servings: 1 serving
Preparation Time: 10 minutes
Time to Cook: 15 minutes

Ingredients
- 1 cup kale leaves (stems removed, torn into bite-sized pieces)
- 1/2 tablespoon olive oil
- 1/4 teaspoon sea salt
- A pinch of black pepper (optional)

Instructions
1. Preheat your oven to 350°F (175°C).
2. Toss the kale leaves with olive oil in a bowl until they are evenly coated.
3. Arrange the kale leaves in a single layer on a baking sheet.
4. Sprinkle sea salt (and black pepper if desired) over the kale.
5. Bake for 10-15 minutes or until the kale is crisp and slightly browned but not burnt. Keep a close eye on them, as they can burn quickly.
6. Remove from the oven and let the Baked Kale Chips cool for a few minutes.
7. Enjoy your homemade crunchy and nutritious kale chips!

Per Serving Calories: 120 Protein: 4g Fat: 7g Salt: 580mg

Zucchini Carrot Fritters

Total Servings: 1 serving
Preparation Time: 15 minutes
Time to Cook: 10 minutes

Ingredients
- 1/2 cup grated zucchini
- 1/2 cup grated carrot
- 1/4 cup chickpea flour
- 1/2 teaspoon ground cumin
- 1/2 teaspoon ground coriander
- A pinch of sea salt
- 1 tablespoon olive oil (for frying)

Instructions
1. Place the grated zucchini and carrot in a clean kitchen or paper towel and squeeze out excess moisture.
2. Combine the grated zucchini, grated carrot, chickpea flour, ground cumin, coriander, and a pinch of sea salt in a bowl. Mix until well combined.
3. Heat olive oil in a non-stick skillet over medium heat.
4. Form the mixture into small patties and place them in the hot skillet.
5. Cook for about 4-5 minutes on each side or until golden brown patties are cooked through.
6. Remove from the skillet and let them cool for a minute.
7. Enjoy your Zucchini Carrot Fritters as a healthy and savory snack or side dish!

Per Serving Calories: 320 Protein: 9g Fat: 14g Salt: 420mg

Roasted Red Pepper Hummus

Total Servings: 1 serving
Preparation Time: 10 minutes
Time to Cook: 0 minutes

Ingredients
- 1/2 cup canned chickpeas (rinsed and drained)
- 1/4 cup roasted red peppers (from a jar, drained)
- 1 tablespoon tahini
- 1 tablespoon olive oil
- 1/2 clove garlic (minced)
- Juice of 1/2 lemon
- A pinch of sea salt

Instructions
1. Combine canned chickpeas, roasted red peppers, tahini, olive oil, minced garlic, lemon juice, and a pinch of sea salt in a food processor.
2. Process until smooth and creamy. If the mixture is too thick, add water to achieve your desired consistency.
3. Transfer the Roasted Red Pepper Hummus to a serving dish.
4. If desired, drizzle with extra olive oil and garnish with chickpeas or chopped fresh herbs.
5. Enjoy your homemade, flavorful hummus with your favorite veggies or whole-grain crackers!

Per Serving Calories: 360 Protein: 9g Fat: 20g Salt: 400mg

Turmeric Chickpea Snack

Total Servings: 1 serving
Preparation Time: 5 minutes
Time to Cook: 15 minutes

Ingredients
- 1/2 cup canned chickpeas (rinsed and drained)
- 1/2 teaspoon olive oil
- 1/2 teaspoon ground turmeric
- 1/4 teaspoon ground cumin
- A pinch of cayenne pepper (optional for heat)
- A pinch of sea salt

Instructions

1. Preheat your oven to 400°F (200°C).

2. In a bowl, toss the chickpeas with olive oil, ground turmeric, ground cumin, cayenne pepper (if desired), and a pinch of sea salt until they are well coated.

3. Spread the seasoned chickpeas on a baking sheet in a single layer.

4. Roast in the oven for about 15 minutes or until the chickpeas are crispy and golden brown. Shake the pan or stir the chickpeas halfway through cooking.

5. Remove from the oven and let the Turmeric Chickpea Snack cool for a few minutes.

6. Enjoy your homemade anti-inflammatory spiced chickpea snack!

Per Serving Calories: 200 Protein: 7g Fat: 6g Salt: 440mg

Cucumber Yogurt Dip

Total Servings: 1 serving
Preparation Time: 10 minutes
Time to Cook: 0 minutes

Ingredients
- 1/2 cup Greek yogurt (unsweetened)
- 1/4 cucumber, finely grated
- 1/2 clove garlic (minced)
- 1/2 teaspoon fresh dill (chopped)
- Juice of 1/4 lemon
- A pinch of sea salt
- Fresh cucumber slices and carrot sticks for dipping (optional)

Instructions

1. Combine Greek yogurt, finely grated cucumber, minced garlic, chopped fresh dill, lemon juice, and a pinch of sea salt in a bowl.

2. Mix until all ingredients are well combined.

3. Transfer the Cucumber Yogurt Dip to a serving bowl.

4. If desired, serve with fresh cucumber slices and carrot sticks for a refreshing and healthy snack.

5. Enjoy your homemade creamy and tangy dip!

Per Serving Calories: 120 Protein: 10g Fat: 4g Salt: 320mg

Cauliflower Buffalo Bites

Total Servings: 1 serving
Preparation Time: 15 minutes
Time to Cook: 20 minutes

Ingredients
- 1/2 cup cauliflower florets
- 1/2 tablespoon olive oil
- 1/4 teaspoon smoked paprika
- 1/4 teaspoon garlic powder
- 1/4 teaspoon onion powder
- 1/4 cup hot sauce (look for a low-sodium option)
- A pinch of sea salt
- Celery sticks and carrot sticks for dipping (optional)

Instructions

1. Preheat your oven to 450°F (230°C).

2. Toss the cauliflower florets in a bowl with olive oil, smoked paprika, garlic powder, onion powder, and a pinch of sea salt until they are evenly coated.

3. Spread the seasoned cauliflower on a baking sheet in a single layer.

4. Roast in the oven for about 20 minutes or until the cauliflower is tender and slightly crispy.

5. While the cauliflower is roasting, mix the hot sauce and a pinch of sea salt in a separate bowl.

6. Remove the roasted cauliflower from the oven and drizzle the hot sauce mixture. Toss to coat the cauliflower in the sauce.

7. Return the cauliflower to the oven and roast for an additional 5 minutes.

8. Remove from the oven and let the Cauliflower Buffalo Bites cool for a few minutes.

9. If desired, serve with celery and carrot sticks for a spicy and satisfying snack

10. Enjoy your homemade anti-inflammatory cauliflower bites!

Per Serving Calories: 180 Protein: 4g Fat: 8g Salt: 600mg

Spiced Edamame Pods

Total Servings: 1 serving
Preparation Time: 10 minutes
Time to Cook: 5 minutes

Ingredients
- 1 cup frozen edamame pods
- 1/2 teaspoon olive oil
- 1/4 teaspoon ground cumin

- 1/4 teaspoon ground coriander
- A pinch of cayenne pepper (optional for heat)
- A pinch of sea salt

Instructions

1. Cook the frozen edamame pods according to the package instructions (usually by boiling or steaming) until they are tender but firm. Drain and set aside.

2. In a skillet, heat olive oil over medium heat.

3. Add the cooked edamame pods to the skillet and sauté for 2-3 minutes.

4. Sprinkle ground cumin, coriander, cayenne pepper (if desired), and a pinch of sea salt over the edamame pods. Toss to coat evenly.

5. Sauté for another 2 minutes or until the edamame pods are lightly browned and fragrant.

6. Remove from heat and let the Spiced Edamame Pods cool for a minute.

7. Enjoy your homemade anti-inflammatory spiced edamame pods as a flavorful snack!

Per Serving Calories: 160 Protein: 13g Fat: 7g Salt: 210mg

Sweet Potato Salsa

Total Servings: 1 serving
Preparation Time: 15 minutes
Time to Cook: 20 minutes

Ingredients

- 1/2 cup sweet potato (peeled and diced)
- 1/4 cup diced red bell pepper
- 1/4 cup diced red onion
- 1/4 cup diced fresh tomatoes
- 1/4 cup fresh cilantro (chopped)
- Juice of 1/2 lime
- A pinch of sea salt

Instructions

1. Steam or boil the diced sweet potato until it›s tender but not mushy. Drain and set aside to cool.

2. In a bowl, combine the cooled sweet potato, diced red bell pepper, diced red onion, diced fresh tomatoes, chopped fresh cilantro, lime juice, and a pinch of sea salt. Mix gently to combine.

3. Refrigerate the Sweet Potato Salsa for at least 15 minutes to allow the flavors to meld.

4. Serve as a topping for grilled chicken or fish or as a side dish with whole-grain crackers or tortilla chips.

5. Enjoy your homemade anti-inflammatory sweet potato salsa!

Per Serving Calories: 150 Protein: 3g Fat: 0.5g Salt: 250mg

Mango Avocado Salsa

Total Servings: 1 serving
Preparation Time: 10 minutes
Time to Cook: 0 minutes

Ingredients

- 1/2 ripe mango (diced)
- 1/2 ripe avocado (diced)
- 1/4 cup diced red onion
- 1/4 cup fresh cilantro (chopped)
- Juice of 1/2 lime
- A pinch of sea salt
- A pinch of black pepper (optional)

Instructions

6. In a bowl, combine the diced mango, avocado, red onion, chopped fresh cilantro, lime juice, a pinch of sea salt, and black pepper (if desired). Gently mix to combine.

7. Refrigerate the Mango Avocado Salsa for at least 10 minutes to allow the flavors to meld.

8. Serve as a topping for grilled chicken or fish or a delicious side dish with whole-grain tortilla chips.

9. Enjoy your homemade anti-inflammatory mango avocado salsa!

Per Serving Calories: 250 Protein: 3 Fat: 15g Salt: 320mg

Beetroot Goat Cheese Crostini

Total Servings: 1 serving
Preparation Time: 15 minutes
Time to Cook: 0 minutes

Ingredients

- 2 slices whole-grain baguette or bread
- 2 tablespoons goat cheese
- 1 small beetroot (cooked and thinly sliced)
- Fresh basil leaves for garnish
- A drizzle of extra virgin olive oil
- A pinch of sea salt
- A pinch of black pepper (optional)

Instructions

1. Toast the whole-grain baguette slices until they are lightly browned.

2. Spread goat cheese evenly on each slice of toasted bread.

3. Arrange the thinly sliced cooked beetroot on top of the goat cheese.

4. Garnish with fresh basil leaves.

5. Drizzle with extra virgin olive oil and sprinkle with a pinch of sea salt (and black pepper if desired).

6. Enjoy your homemade anti-inflammatory Beetroot Goat Cheese Crostini as a flavorful appetizer or snack!

Per Serving Calories: 240 Protein: 8g Fat: 8g Salt: 480mg

Tomato Basil Bruschetta

Total Servings: 1 serving
Preparation Time: 15 minutes
Time to Cook: 0 minutes

Ingredients

- 2 slices whole-grain baguette or bread
- 1 small tomato (diced)
- 1/4 cup fresh basil leaves (chopped)
- 1/2 clove garlic (minced)
- A drizzle of extra virgin olive oil
- A pinch of sea salt
- A pinch of black pepper (optional)

Instructions

1. Toast the whole-grain baguette slices until they are lightly browned.

2. Combine diced tomato, chopped fresh basil leaves, minced garlic, and a pinch of sea salt in a bowl. Mix well.

3. Place the tomato basil mixture evenly on top of each slice of toasted bread.

4. Drizzle with extra virgin olive oil and sprinkle with a pinch of sea salt (and black pepper if desired).

5. Enjoy your homemade anti-inflammatory Tomato Basil Bruschetta as a delightful appetizer or snack!

Per Serving Calories: 180 Protein: 5g Fat: 5g Salt: 340mg

Prosciutto Asparagus Wraps

Total Servings: 1 serving
Preparation Time: 10 minutes
Time to Cook: 5 minutes

Ingredients

- 4 asparagus spears
- 2 thin slices of prosciutto
- A drizzle of extra virgin olive oil
- A pinch of black pepper (optional)
- Fresh lemon zest for garnish
- Toothpicks for securing

Instructions

1. Trim the tough ends of the asparagus spears.

2. Wrap each asparagus spear with a slice of prosciutto.

3. Heat a drizzle of extra virgin olive oil in a skillet over medium-high heat.

4. Place the prosciutto-wrapped asparagus in the skillet

and sauté for about 3-5 minutes, turning occasionally, until the asparagus is tender and the prosciutto is crispy.

5. Remove from heat and sprinkle with a pinch of black pepper (and fresh lemon zest if desired).

6. Secure each Prosciutto Asparagus Wrap with a toothpick.

7. Enjoy your homemade anti-inflammatory prosciutto-wrapped asparagus as a tasty appetizer or side dish!

Per Serving Calories: 160 Protein: 9g Fat: 10g Salt: 560mg

Quinoa Mini Peppers

Total Servings: 1 serving
Preparation Time: 15 minutes
Time to Cook: 20 minutes

Ingredients

- 3 mini bell peppers (assorted colors)
- 1/4 cup quinoa (rinsed and drained)
- 1/2 cup vegetable broth (low sodium)
- 1/4 cup cherry tomatoes (halved)
- 1/4 cup cucumber (diced)
- 1 tablespoon fresh parsley (chopped)
- A drizzle of extra virgin olive oil
- A pinch of sea salt
- A pinch of black pepper (optional)

Instructions

1. Preheat your oven to 375°F (190°C).

2. Cut the tops off the mini bell peppers and remove the seeds.

3. In a small saucepan, combine quinoa and vegetable broth. Bring to a boil, then reduce heat to low, cover, and simmer for 15-20 minutes or until quinoa is cooked and liquid is absorbed.

4. While the quinoa is cooking, place the hollowed-out mini bell peppers on a baking sheet, drizzle with some extra virgin olive oil, and roast in the oven for about 10 minutes or until slightly softened.

5. Combine the cooked quinoa, halved cherry tomatoes, diced cucumber, chopped fresh parsley, and a pinch of sea salt in a bowl. Mix well.

6. Stuff the roasted mini bell peppers with the quinoa mixture.

7. Season with a pinch of black pepper (and extra olive oil if desired).

8. Enjoy your homemade anti-inflammatory Quinoa Mini Peppers as a colorful and nutritious appetizer or snack!

Per Serving Calories: 280Protein: 8g Fat: 8g Salt: 400mg

Herb Marinated Olives

Total Servings: 1 serving
Preparation Time: 10 minutes
Time to Cook: 0 minutes

Ingredients

- 1/4 cup mixed olives (pitted)
- 1/2 teaspoon extra virgin olive oil
- 1/2 teaspoon fresh thyme leaves (chopped)
- 1/2 teaspoon fresh rosemary leaves (chopped)
- 1/2 teaspoon fresh oregano leaves (chopped)
- 1/2 clove garlic (minced)
- A pinch of red pepper flakes (optional)
- A pinch of lemon zest (optional)

Instructions

1. In a bowl, combine mixed olives, extra virgin olive oil, chopped fresh thyme, chopped fresh rosemary, chopped fresh oregano, minced garlic, red pepper flakes (if desired), and lemon zest (if desired). Mix well.

2. Allow the Herb Marinated Olives to sit at room temperature for 10 minutes to let the flavors meld.

3. Enjoy your homemade anti-inflammatory Herb Marinated Olives as a savory and aromatic snack or appetizer!

Per Serving Calories: 130 Protein: 1g Fat: 13g Salt: 600mg

Sweet Potato Fries

Total Servings: 1 serving
Preparation Time: 15 minutes
Time to Cook: 20 minutes

Ingredients
- 1 small sweet potato (cut into fries)
- 1/2 tablespoon olive oil
- 1/4 teaspoon paprika
- 1/4 teaspoon garlic powder
- A pinch of sea salt
- A pinch of black pepper (optional)

Instructions

1. Preheat your oven to 425°F (220°C).

2. Toss the sweet potato fries with olive oil, paprika, garlic powder, a pinch of sea salt, and black pepper (if desired) until they are evenly coated.

3. Arrange the seasoned sweet potato fries on a baking sheet in a single layer.

4. Roast in the preheated oven for about 20 minutes or until the sweet potato fries are crispy and golden brown, turning them halfway through cooking.

5. Remove from the oven and let the Sweet Potato Fries cool for a minute.

6. Enjoy your homemade anti-inflammatory Sweet Potato Fries as a tasty and nutritious side dish or snack!

Per Serving Calories: 260 Protein: 3g Fat: 7g Salt: 340mg

Spicy Almond Dates

Total Servings: 1 serving
Preparation Time: 5 minutes

Time to Cook: 0 minutes

Ingredients
- 4 pitted Medjool dates
- 8 almonds
- A pinch of cayenne pepper
- A pinch of ground cinnamon
- A pinch of sea salt

Instructions

1. Carefully open each pitted Medjool date and insert two almonds into each date.

2. Combine a pinch of cayenne pepper, some ground cinnamon, and a pinch of sea salt in a small bowl.

3. Roll each almond-stuffed date in the spicy seasoning mixture until coated.

4. Enjoy your homemade anti-inflammatory Spicy Almond Dates as a sweet and spicy snack!

Per Serving Calories: 180 Protein: 3g Fat: 6g Salt: 90mg

Turmeric Popcorn

Total Servings: 1 serving
Preparation Time: 5 minutes
Time to Cook: 5 minutes

Ingredients
- 1/4 cup popcorn kernels
- 1/2 tablespoon coconut oil
- 1/2 teaspoon ground turmeric
- A pinch of sea salt
- A pinch of black pepper (optional)

Instructions

1. In a large pot, heat the coconut oil over medium-high heat.

2. Add a few popcorn kernels to the pot and cover it with a lid.

3. Once the test kernels pop, please remove them and add the remaining popcorn kernels to the pot.

4. Sprinkle ground turmeric evenly over the kernels.

5. Cover the pot with a lid and shake it gently to ensure the turmeric coats the kernels.

6. Continue to cook, shaking the pot occasionally to prevent burning, until the popping slows to about 2 seconds between pops. Remove from heat.

7. Sprinkle a pinch of sea salt (and black pepper if desired) over the Turmeric Popcorn and toss gently to coat.

8. Enjoy your homemade anti-inflammatory Turmeric Popcorn as a flavorful and crunchy snack!

Per Serving Calories: 120 Protein: 3g Fat: 5g Salt: 160mg

Cucumber Dill Ceviche

Total Servings: 1 serving
Preparation Time: 15 minutes
Time to Cook: 0 minutes

Ingredients

- 1/2 cucumber (peeled and diced)
- 1/4 red onion (finely chopped)
- 1/2 small tomato (diced)
- 1/4 cup fresh cilantro (chopped)
- 1/2 lime (juiced)
- 1/2 teaspoon fresh dill (chopped)
- A pinch of sea salt
- A pinch of black pepper (optional)

Instructions

1. In a bowl, combine diced cucumber, finely chopped red onion, tomato, chopped fresh cilantro, lime juice, chopped fresh dill, a pinch of sea salt, and black pepper (if desired).

2. Mix well to combine all the ingredients.

3. Refrigerate the Cucumber Dill Ceviche for about 10 minutes to allow the flavors to meld.

4. Enjoy your homemade anti-inflammatory Cucumber Dill Ceviche as a refreshing, tangy snack or appetizer!

Per Serving Calories: 70 Protein: 2g Fat: 0g Salt: 320mg

Stuffed Mushroom Dip

Total Servings: 1 serving
Preparation Time: 15 minutes
Time to Cook: 25 minutes

Ingredients

- 4 large white button mushrooms
- 1 tablespoon olive oil
- 1 clove garlic (minced)
- 1/4 cup spinach (finely chopped)
- 2 tablespoons cream cheese (or dairy-free alternative)
- 1 tablespoon grated Parmesan cheese (or dairy-free alternative)
- A pinch of sea salt
- A pinch of black pepper (optional)

Instructions

1. Preheat your oven to 350°F (175°C).

2. Carefully remove the stems from the mushrooms and set them aside. You'll use them in the filling.

3. In a skillet, heat olive oil over medium heat. Add minced garlic and chopped mushroom stems. Sauté until the mushrooms are tender and the liquid evaporates about 5 minutes.

4. Add chopped spinach to the skillet and sauté for another 2-3 minutes until it wilts. Remove from heat.

5. Mix cream cheese (or dairy-free alternative), grated Parmesan cheese (or dairy-free alternative), and the sautéed mushroom and spinach mixture in a small bowl. Season with a pinch of sea salt and black pepper if desired.

6. Stuff each mushroom cap with the filling mixture.

7. Place the stuffed mushrooms on a baking sheet and bake in the oven for about 20 minutes or until the mushrooms are tender and the tops are lightly browned.

8. Enjoy your homemade anti-inflammatory Stuffed Mushroom Dip as a warm and savory appetizer!

Per Serving Calories: 220 Protein: 6g Fat: 18g Salt: 260mg

Smoked Salmon Rounds

Total Servings: 1 serving
Preparation Time: 10 minutes
Time to Cook: 0 minutes

Ingredients

- 4 slices smoked salmon
- 2 tablespoons cream cheese (or dairy-free alternative)
- 1/4 small cucumber (sliced into thin rounds)
- Fresh dill sprigs for garnish
- A pinch of black pepper (optional)
- A squeeze of lemon juice (optional)

Instructions

1. Lay out the smoked salmon slices on a clean surface.

2. Spread a thin layer of cream cheese (or dairy-free alternative) evenly over each slice of smoked salmon.

3. Place a cucumber round on top of each cream cheese-covered salmon slice.

4. Garnish with fresh dill sprigs.

5. Season with a pinch of black pepper and a squeeze of lemon juice if desired.

6. Enjoy your homemade anti-inflammatory Smoked Salmon Rounds as an elegant and refreshing appetizer!

Per Serving: Calories: 170 Protein: 12g Fat: 12g Salt: 430mg

Pistachio Energy Bites

Total Servings: 1 serving
Preparation Time: 10 minutes
Time to Cook: 0 minutes

Ingredients

- 1/4 cup shelled pistachio nuts
- 2 Medjool dates (pitted)
- 1 tablespoon rolled oats
- 1/4 teaspoon ground cinnamon
- A pinch of sea salt
- A pinch of unsweetened cocoa powder (optional)

- A pinch of grated orange zest (optional)

Instructions

1. In a food processor, combine shelled pistachio nuts, pitted Medjool dates, rolled oats, ground cinnamon, a pinch of sea salt, and any optional ingredients (cocoa powder or grated orange zest). Process until the mixture comes together and forms a sticky dough.

2. Remove the dough from the food processor and roll it into bite-sized balls.

3. Optionally, roll the Pistachio Energy Bites in additional crushed pistachios for added texture.

4. Enjoy your homemade anti-inflammatory Pistachio Energy Bites as a wholesome and energizing snack!

Per Serving: Calories: 280 Protein: 6g Fat: 13g Salt: 60mg

Baked Eggplant Chips

Total Servings: 1 serving
Preparation Time: 15 minutes
Time to Cook: 20 minutes

Ingredients

- 1 small eggplant
- 1 tablespoon olive oil
- 1/4 teaspoon smoked paprika
- 1/4 teaspoon garlic powder
- A pinch of sea salt
- A pinch of black pepper (optional)
- Fresh parsley for garnish (optional)

Instructions

1. Preheat your oven to 425°F (220°C).

2. Slice the eggplant into thin rounds, about 1/4 inch thick.

3. In a bowl, toss the eggplant rounds with olive oil, smoked paprika, garlic powder, a pinch of sea salt, and black pepper (if desired) until they are evenly coated.

4. Arrange the seasoned eggplant rounds on a baking sheet in a single layer.

5. Bake in the preheated oven for about 15-20 minutes, turning them over halfway through cooking, until the eggplant chips are crispy and lightly browned.

6. Remove from the oven and let the Baked Eggplant Chips cool for a minute.

7. Garnish with fresh parsley (if desired).

8. Enjoy your homemade anti-inflammatory Baked Eggplant Chips as a crunchy and nutritious snack!

Per Serving Calories: 150 Protein: 2g Fat: 11g Salt: 120mg

Yogurt Herb Dip

Total Servings: 1 serving
Preparation Time: 5 minutes
Time to Cook: 0 minutes

Ingredients

- 1/2 cup Greek yogurt (or dairy-free alternative)
- 1/2 teaspoon fresh dill (chopped)
- 1/2 teaspoon fresh chives (chopped)
- 1/4 teaspoon fresh parsley (chopped)
- 1/4 teaspoon fresh mint leaves (chopped)
- 1/2 clove garlic (minced)
- A pinch of sea salt
- A pinch of black pepper (optional)
- A squeeze of lemon juice (optional)

Instructions

1. In a bowl, combine Greek yogurt (or dairy-free alternative), chopped fresh dill, chopped fresh chives, chopped fresh parsley, chopped fresh mint leaves, minced garlic, a pinch of sea salt, black pepper (if desired), and a squeeze of lemon juice (if desired). Mix well.

2. Refrigerate the Yogurt Herb Dip for about 10 minutes to allow the flavors to meld.

3. Enjoy your homemade anti-inflammatory Yogurt Herb Dip as a creamy and herby dip for your Baked Eggplant Chips!

Per Serving Calories: 90 Protein: 10g Fat: 4g Salt: 320mg

Tuna Avocado Wraps

Total Servings: 1 serving
Preparation Time: 10 minutes
Time to Cook: 0 minutes

Ingredients

- 1 small whole-grain tortilla (or gluten-free alternative)
- 1/2 avocado (sliced)
- 1/2 can (3.5 oz) tuna in water (drained)
- 1/4 cup red bell pepper (sliced into thin strips)
- 1/4 cup cucumber (sliced into thin strips)
- 1/4 cup carrot (sliced into thin strips)
- 2 tablespoons plain Greek yogurt (or dairy-free alternative)
- A pinch of sea salt
- A pinch of black pepper (optional)

Instructions

1. Lay the whole-grain tortilla flat on a clean surface.

2. Spread a layer of sliced avocado evenly over the tortilla.

3. Place the drained tuna in the center of the tortilla, on top of the avocado.

4. Arrange the sliced red bell pepper, cucumber, and carrot strips on the tuna.

5. Drizzle plain Greek yogurt (or dairy-free alternative) over the veggies.

6. Season with a pinch of sea salt and black pepper (if desired).

7. Carefully fold in the sides of the tortilla and then roll it up from the bottom, creating a wrap.

8. Slice the Tuna Avocado Wrap in half, if desired.

9. Enjoy your homemade anti-inflammatory Tuna Avocado Wrap as a quick and nutritious meal!

Per Serving Calories: 330 Protein: 22g Fat: 15g Salt: 510mg

Beet Walnut Hummus

Total Servings: 1 serving
Preparation Time: 10 minutes
Time to Cook: 0 minutes

Ingredients
- 1 small cooked beetroot (peeled and diced)
- 1/4 cup walnuts
- 2 tablespoons tahini
- 1 tablespoon lemon juice
- 1/2 clove garlic (minced)
- A pinch of sea salt
- A pinch of ground cumin (optional)
- A pinch of paprika (optional)
- Fresh parsley leaves for garnish (optional)

Instructions

1. In a food processor, combine the diced cooked beetroot, walnuts, tahini, lemon juice, minced garlic, a pinch of sea salt, and ground cumin (if desired).

2. Process the ingredients until you achieve a smooth and creamy consistency. You may need to scrape down the sides of the processor and blend again to ensure everything is well combined.

3. If the hummus is too thick, add a teaspoon of water at a time and blend until it reaches your desired consistency.

4. Taste the Beet Walnut Hummus and adjust the seasonings if needed, adding more salt or lemon juice to taste.

5. Optionally, sprinkle with paprika and garnish with fresh parsley leaves.

6. Enjoy your homemade anti-inflammatory Beet Walnut Hummus as a vibrant, nutritious dip or spread!

Per Serving Calories: 340 Protein: 9g Fat: 30g Salt: 360mg

Chapter 11:
30-Day Meal Plan
Week 1

Day	Breakfast	A.m/P.m Snack	Lunch	Dinner
Monday	Turmeric Scramble	Herb-Roasted Chicken	Grilled Lemon Herb Chicken	Lemon Herb Poached Cod
Tuesday	Berry Quinoa Bowl	Lemon Garlic Roast Turkey	Garlic Rosemary Lamb Chops	Cilantro-Lime Octopus
Wednesday	Avocado Tomato Toast	Orange Ginger Glazed Duck	Turmeric Glazed Salmon	Herbed Lobster Tails
Thursday	Green Spinach Smoothie	Cilantro-Lime Chicken Thighs	Beef Stir-Fry with Ginger	Garlic Herb Haddock
Friday	Chia Almond Pudding	Balsamic-Honey Glazed Quail	Balsamic Turkey Tenderloin	Sesame Wasabi Tuna
Saturday	Sweet Potato Hash	Mango Turkey Burgers	Mediterranean Shrimp Skewers	Citrus-Marinated Shrimp Skewers
Sunday	Coconut Yogurt Parfait	Rosemary Roast Cornish Hens	Pork Tenderloin with Chutney	Cucumber Marinated Salmon

Week 2

Day	Breakfast	A.m/P.m Snack	Lunch	Dinner
Monday	Salmon Avocado Wrap	Lemongrass Coconut Curry	Spiced Turkey Lettuce Wraps	Cajun Crawfish Boil
Tuesday	Almond Banana Oats	Garlic-Herb Drumsticks	Herbed Chicken Skillet	Blackened Snapper Mango
Wednesday	Spinach Mushroom Frittata	Tarragon Roast Game Hens	Lemon Pepper Tuna	Lemon-Garlic Crab Legs
Thursday	Tofu Breakfast Tacos	Chili-Lime Turkey Skewers	Lime Cilantro Grilled Mahi-Mahi	Turmeric Coconut Shrimp
Friday	Mango Turmeric Blend	Apricot Glazed Chicken Wings	Coconut-Curry Tilapia	Mango Avocado Tuna Salad
Saturday	Zucchini Casserole	Sesame-Ginger Turkey Stir-Fry	Sesame Tuna Steak	Ginger Soy Sea Bass
Sunday	Almond Butter Sandwich	Basil Grilled Quail	Paprika Garlic Swordfish	Mediterranean Sardines

Week 3

Day	Breakfast	A.m/P.m Snack	Lunch	Dinner
Monday	Quinoa Kale Bowl	Curry Chicken Drumettes	Citrus-Marinated Grilled Halibut	Lemon-Herb Baked Trout
Tuesday	Anti-Inflammatory Burrito	Honey Mustard Turkey	Spicy Sriracha Sardines	Spicy Chili-Lime Prawns
Wednesday	Coconut Chia Mango	Paprika Herb Chicken Thighs	Cajun Blackened Catfish	Curry Lamb Kebabs
Thursday	Spinach Pepper Muffins	Pomegranate Glazed Chicken Legs	Turmeric Lentil Soup	Roasted Veggie Quinoa Salad
Friday	Turmeric Scramble	Herb-Roasted Chicken	Grilled Lemon Herb Chicken	Lemon Herb Poached Cod
Saturday	Berry Quinoa Bowl	Lemon Garlic Roast Turkey	Garlic Rosemary Lamb Chops	Cilantro-Lime Octopus
Sunday	Avocado Tomato Toast	Orange Ginger Glazed Duck	Turmeric Glazed Salmon	Herbed Lobster Tails

Week 4

Days	Breakfast	A.m/P.m Snack	Lunch	Dinner
Monday	Blueberry Pancakes	Basil Grilled Quail	Balsamic-Honey Glazed Quail	Pomegranate Glazed Chicken Legs
Tuesday	Cinnamon Quinoa Porridge	Apricot Sage Turkey Meatballs	Curry Chicken Drumettes	Lemon Herb Poached Cod
Wednesday	Berry Yogurt Mix	Garlic-Herb Drumsticks	Honey Mustard Turkey	Herbed Lobster Tails
Thursday	Veggie Burritos	Turmeric Lentil Soup	Paprika Herb Chicken Thighs	Cajun Crawfish Boil
Friday	Golden Milk Oats	Rosemary Roast Cornish Hens	Spiced Chicken Tenders	Blackened Snapper Mango
Saturday	Spinach Tomato Quesadilla	Sesame-Crusted Chicken Tenders	Cranberry-Pecan Turkey	Lemon-Herb Baked Trout
Sunday	Matcha Green Smoothie	Mango Avocado Turkey Salad	Pomegranate Glazed Chicken Legs	Spicy Chili-Lime Prawns

Week 5

Days	Breakfast	A.m/P.m Snack	Lunch	Dinner
Monday	Cauliflower Hash Browns	Sesame-Ginger Turkey Stir-Fry	Herbed Turkey Meatloaf	Curry Lamb Kebabs
Tuesday	Acai Berry Bowl	Basil Grilled Quail	Lemon Dill Whitefish	Dijon Pork Chops

Conclusion

In the final pages of the Anti-Inflammatory Diet Plan Cookbook, we'd like to extend our heartfelt gratitude to you, the reader. Your commitment to your health and well-being is commendable, and we hope this cookbook has served as a valuable companion on your journey to vibrant health.

Embarking on a path to better health can be challenging, and we understand that. We recognize the challenges you've faced, the times you've questioned your choices, and the moments when your motivation waned. Yet, here you are, having taken the steps to embrace an anti-inflammatory lifestyle, you should be immensely proud.

As you've discovered through the pages of this cookbook, the anti-inflammatory diet is not just about what you eat; it's a holistic approach to wellness. It's about nourishing your body with the right foods, fostering a deep connection between mind and body, and finding the balance that works uniquely for you.

But we understand that even the most dedicated individuals may occasionally need a helping hand or a word of encouragement. That's why we encourage you to seek support from friends, family, a healthcare provider, or online communities dedicated to the anti-inflammatory lifestyle. Share your successes and struggles because there is strength in society and in knowing you are not alone on this journey.

Remember that your journey is unique, and progress may not always be linear. There may be detours and obstacles, but every step forward is a victory. Celebrate your achievements, no matter how small they seem, because each one is a testament to your commitment to living healthier, happier lives.

In closing, we want to leave you with a simple yet profound message: Your health is worth it. The energy, vitality, and overall well-being that come with an anti-inflammatory lifestyle are priceless. Keep believing in yourself, exploring new recipes and flavors, and nurturing your body with the love it deserves.

Thank you for allowing us to join your journey toward a healthier, more vibrant you. We wish you continued success, happiness, and boundless health on this incredible path of the anti-inflammatory diet.

Made in United States
Troutdale, OR
10/17/2023

13770804R10058